DANIEL ISLAND

Bird
Fellingham Towne

Comings
Land

Creek
Turkey
Dukes
Hunt
Brown
Dryo

Bodicot
Faulkner
Halton
Cockfield
Grimball
Mr. Suloan

Bar Bull
Smith
King

Wood
Perryman
new Land
Jackson
Lund

Tingley
Buckler
Lewis

Codner
Cap St Tho
Jacks
Isl

Jefford
Jefford Toure
Chamber
Colliton
William
new Son

Marshall
Bryan
Owen
West
Neasler

Benlagrois
Simons
Steirke

Nottle
Morton
Lodge
D. Trivillion
Tender
Col Godfry
Cartwright
Beadon
Gray
Green
Hopson
Land rugs
Coming

M. Foster

DANIEL ISLAND

Michael K. Dahlman and Michael K. Dahlman Jr.

ARCADIA
PUBLISHING

Copyright © 2006 by Michael K. Dahlman and Michael K. Dahlman Jr.
ISBN 978-0-7385-4357-4

Published by Arcadia Publishing,
Charleston SC, Chicago IL, Portsmouth NH, San Francisco CA

Printed in the United States

Library of Congress control number: 2006936984

For all general information contact Arcadia Publishing at:
Telephone 843-853-2070
Fax 843-853-0044
E-Mail sales@arcadiapublishing.com
For customer service and orders:
Toll-Free 1-888-313-2665

Visit us on the Internet at www.arcadiapublishing.com

The authors will donate 20 percent of their proceeds from the sale of this book to the Cainhoy community.

This book is dedicated to our Heavenly Father for the graces that have shepherded it to its completion, as well as to all those who have lived and worked on Daniel Island and who have shared in the creation of its 5,000 years of history.

Contents

APPRECIATION

This History of Daniel Island would not have been possible without the support and encouragement of a good number of people.

Our editors, Adam Ferrell and Jim Kempert, for their persistence without which the stories and information would have remained a great collection of trivia and unpublished factoids.

Rev. David Reilly, for his friendship and mentorship and for the profound belief in what we set out to complete.

Bob Tuten, for the hours of time he spent sharing his life with us and making so much of what we found on Daniel Island come alive.

Matt Sloan and Julie Dombrowski of the Daniel Island Company, for their endless support and access to all areas of Daniel Island.

Ralph Bailey, Autumn Morrison, Brett Livingston, and Charlie Philips of Brockington and Associates, for their insights, patience, and helping us understand the historical and archeological context of their work on Daniel Island.

Rev. Benjamin Dennis, Phillip Simons, and Fred Lincoln, for hours of personal stories of what life was like on Daniel Island from the mid 1920s to the mid 1990s, as well as tremendous insights into the meaning of what we are seeing today.

Peter Lawson-Johnston and the staff of the Harry F. Guggenheim Foundation for their hospitality and willingness to open their doors to us throughout the writing of this book.

Philip Daniel and Ken Daniel, for their insights into Daniel family history.

Ross Taylor and the staff of the Cooper Library map collection room, University of South Carolina.

Richard Harris and the staff of the state Department of Archives and History.

Nick Butler, head of special collections, and the staff of the Carolina Room, Charleston County Public Library.

Shan Burkhalter and Jeff Payne of the National Oceanic and Atmospheric Administration Coastal Services Center, Charleston.

Mike Coker and the staff of the South Carolina Historical Society.

And mostly to our family, who suffered through countless weekends and nights of putting this all together.

Post holes outline the remnants of an early 1500s circular Native American dwelling that was investigated by archeologists along Ralston Creek. Circular structures were usually built to support a temporary living site, normally used in the winter months on Daniel Island. (Courtesy Brockington and Associates.)

1. Native Americans on Etiwan Island

According to early land grant records of the Carolina colony, the Native American residents of Daniel Island called their home Etiwan Island and lived along its marshes and on the banks of the Wando River. Many sites on Daniel Island have been identified as locations of Native American settlements, but most have been significantly disturbed by nearly a century of agricultural activity, especially the deep plowing of the land during the island's truck farming days.

"Locations that were the best places to live on Daniel Island prior to the arrival of Europeans are the best places to live now," according to Native American expert Brent Livingston. Nearly every excavated site has revealed Indian relics, including some of the oldest ceramics found anywhere in North America. Archeologists have uncovered arrowheads that date from 10,000 years ago, along with pottery shards that indicate Etiwan Island (also spelled Ittiuan or Iittyman) was an important living area from at least 2500 b.c.

Native American culture has been grouped into eras that are defined by changes in hunting, trading, and production of tools for cooking and hunting. The Archaic Period spans the time from 8000 b.c. to 1500 b.c. when hunting and gathering followed seasonal patterns in an area that stretched locally from the coast to the Piedmont. Large shell mounds, or shell middens, from the end of this period indicate that areas along the coast and major rivers were occupied for extended periods.

Between 1500 b.c. and 1000 a.d., the Woodland Period, hunting and gathering continued while villages began to be occupied for years at a time, accompanied by organized agriculture. It was during this time that clay and ceramic vessels were first made to cook and store food, leaving an archeological record that survives to the present day.

By 1000 a.d., the beginning of the Mississippian Period, corn was grown as a cultivated crop, complicated social structures between tribes existed, and trading took place over distances of hundreds of miles. Many of these Indian trading routes became the first roads of the European colonies, and

Good locations were used over and over again by the Native Americans. These two circular pits were hearths that predate the building of the rectangular structure by several hundred years. Rectangular buildings were usually constructed for year-round occupation, supporting other evidence that by the time the colony was settled the Etiwan Indians were living year-round on Daniel Island. (Courtesy Brockington and Associates.)

today some of the same routes are followed by modern highways. U.S. Highway 17 is a good example, as is the layout of Interstate 26 between Charleston and Columbia.

Protection of the Historical Treasury on Daniel Island

The historical significance of Daniel Island can be attributed both to its location near the first major European settlement in the Carolinas and to its relative isolation from the pressures of development. The importance of this relatively undisturbed land is well understood by archaeologists, and present-day development is carefully planned to respect this historical treasure. The South Carolina state historical preservation officer, the U.S. Army Corps of Engineers Charleston District, and the Office of Coastal Resource Management work closely with the Daniel Island Company to provide oversight in areas of potential historical significance and grant final approval before development is allowed to proceed.

The first limited archeological survey of Daniel Island was conducted by Michael Trinkley, the archaeologist for the South Carolina Department of Transportation, in 1978 as a condition of permitting for Interstate 526, the Mark Clark Highway, where it crosses Daniel Island. A more comprehensive survey was performed in 1994 by Brockington and Associates, a cultural consulting company whose staff is composed of archaeologists and historians, as a permitting requirement before development of the island started. The two surveys preliminarily evaluated 34 sites for their potential historical significance. Of these, 13 were deemed important enough to be considered potentially eligible for inclusion in the National Register of Historic Places. This finding of "potentially eligible" requires further investigation before development can take place.

16th Century Indian Village

The site of the Indian Village was one of the areas that merited additional archaeological investigations. The clay soil at the site preserved many relics and features, which provide a unique look into the lives of these early inhabitants. Four structures were identified by the remains of post holes.

Garbage or disposal pits reveal what types of gathering and hunting took place during a site's lifetime. A site on Ralston Creek that underwent extensive excavation had several refuse pits that helped to date the site from 1500 to 1550. Pictured are, from left to right, corn cobs, peach pits, and hickory nuts. (Courtesy Brockington and Associates.)

Shards, or pieces of pottery or ceramic, are a primary method archeologists use to date a site. Native Americans started to make clay pottery around 2500 B.C. and there are numerous sites on Daniel Island that contain shards that date from these earliest pottery workings. These shards, found at a Native American site near the Wando River, are classified as "complicated stamped" and date from the late Mississippian period, 1400-1500. (Courtesy Brockington and Associates.)

Refuse pits revealed that the Native Americans cultivated corn, gathered hickory nuts, hunted deer, and fished in the local waters. Acorns from the many oak trees on the island were a source of cooking oil and were also ground into a type of flour that produced a flat bread. The Indians also gathered oysters from the stream banks, leaving their shells in the refuse pits and also piling them over time in one location, creating the large shell midden nearby. Other contents of the refuse pits indicate that the inhabitants were engaged in active trade with other tribes, some as far as hundreds of miles away. A large number of peach pits were also found. Peaches were considered a delicacy and were brought to North America by the Spaniards, who had established a colonial presence at Santa Elena (Parris Island) to the south in 1526 and at San Miguel de Gualdape to the north from 1556 to 1587. There were also a significant number of raccoon skeletons that bore the marks typically associated with skinning and fur trade. Raccoon pelts were not customarily used by Native Americans, so it is thought that the pelts were being traded to the Spaniards in exchange for other goods.

Brockington and Associate's Brent Livingston conducted many archeological digs on Daniel Island and said the site represents a year-round dwelling that was occupied around 1550. Sites such as this one were normally occupied for five to ten years before the nearby fields were exhausted and new ones had to be opened up for cultivation. The presence of Native American artifacts at nearly every site investigated, especially along the marshes, rivers, and creeks of Daniel Island, strongly points to semi-permanent occupation. Those who lived here probably used canoes or dugouts to navigate between settlements and food-gathering areas. The refuse pits at the Indian Village also indicate that these early inhabitants often hunted deer, which was very important both for its meat and for its skins. Bones from several local species of fish were also found.

The buried remains of a Native American were uncovered on Daniel Island in 2004. The Catawba Indian Nation, located in Rock Hill, South Carolina, works closely with developers in the southeast when Indian remains are found to ensure that proper respect is paid to the location and that the remains are handled in a manner consistent with Native American beliefs. A Catawba Shaman, or spiritual leader, was present when the remains were moved and reburied on Daniel Island in an area that will not be developed. Special care was taken to retain the geographical alignment of the body.

Interestingly, the Catawba Nation has had a long and supportive relationship with the residents of the Carolinas. In 1711, they fought with the British against the Tuscarora of North Carolina during an uprising that

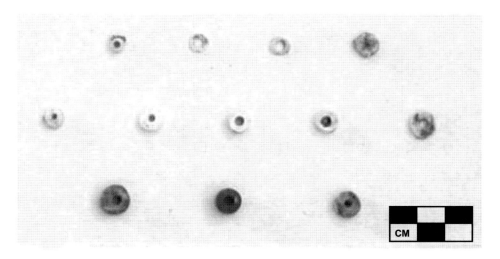

Spanish and English settlers brought glass beads to America. The beads were traded along with axes, hoes, and knives for furs, corn, and deer meat. These beads were found on a Daniel Island Indian settlement that dates to 1550 and are most likely Spanish in origin. (Courtesy Brockington and Associates.)

Shell middens are circular mounds of oyster, clam, and conch shells created by Native Americans beginning around 2000 B.C. They are believed to be refuse dumps associated with villages, although some are associated with ceremonial sites. Most were plundered by early colonists to make lime for cement and mortar. This midden is located along the Wando River near the Wando Bridge.

was instigated by the French and Spanish. They aligned with other native tribes and fought against the colonists during the Yemassee War in 1715, but were essential allies of the colonists in their fight against the British and Cherokee in the Revolutionary War.

Arrival of the English Settlers

When the English settled the present-day Charleston area in the late 1600s, the large social network of the Cofitachequi that the Spanish explorer De Soto had found in the 1540s had been decimated by smallpox, a European disease that the Native Americans had no resistance to. Instead, the English found a loose confederation of tribes in the area who were very friendly to them. The Spanish had formed alliances with the Westo tribe, and the local Indian nations were at war with them. With Spanish guns and support, the Westos often plundered other tribes' villages. From the first contacts along the Carolina coast, the natives saw the English as a way to counter the Spanish influence and defend themselves against the Westos.

Dr. Henry Woodward had joined the first settlers as they traveled from Barbados to Carolina and was fluent in many Native American languages. He was able to act as translator during crucial early meetings with the local tribes and also established contact with the remnants of the Cofitachiequi Nation, which was a 14-day march inland along what is today Interstate 26. A loose confederation of protection was established as early as September 1670, just six months after the *Carolina* landed at Bulls Bay. In a letter from William Owen to Lord Ashley, Owen stated that the nations of the "Edistah, Asha-po, Combohe, Wando, Ituan, Seweh and Sehee promised to muster over 1000 bowmen" should the Spanish threaten the fledgling colony. These nations also provided accurate and timely intelligence of the Spanish and were to be key allies of the English for the next 100 years.

Locally, the Kiawah were occupying the land at Albemarle Point and the lower reaches of the Ashley River, and moved to present-day Kiawah Island after giving lands along the Ashley to the English. The Etiwan Indians were mainly settled on Daniel Island, with territory extending up to present-day Moncks Corner. To the east of Daniel Island and extending to the Santee

Whelk shells were often used as tools to scoop, dig, and slice. These shells were recovered from the Ralston Creek site. (Courtesy Brockington and Associates.)

This 1963 composite aerial photograph of Daniel Island shows the locations of sites where archeologists have uncovered Native American artifacts. Sites along the Wando River and Ralston Creek contain ceramic evidence of extended occupation from 2500 B.C. to the settlement of the Carolina colony. Sites along the Cooper River and the marshes to the south and west of the island reflect a more limited occupation, from 1000 B.C. to 1100 A.D., with the exception of the Jackson plantation site, which has artifacts similar to those found along the Wando. Shaded areas contained a significantly high number of ceramic artifacts. (Photographs courtesy USDA.)

River were the Seewee. The Coosaw inhabited the area to the north and west of the Ashley River. In addition to the military support they provided, these Indian nations also supplied the first colonists with deer meat and corn, without which survival during the first years would have been extraordinarily difficult. The storms encountered by the ships during their journey from England had ruined much of their seed grain, and an early and severe "blast," or frost, prevented many of their crops from reaching harvest.

The colonists were known to share land with the Native Americans and several plats from the early 1700s refer to land occupied by Indians. The governing laws of the colony forbade any settler from obtaining land directly from the Indian nations by trade or favor. It was also strictly prescribed that lands were to be purchased from the Indian nations by representatives of the Carolina colony. In August 1684, a series of conveyances transferred land from the nations of the Wimbee, Stonoh, Combahee, St. Helena, Kussah, and "various Indian Tribes" to the Lords Proprietors. By the middle of the 18th century however, very few Native Americans remained in the Lowcountry of the Carolinas.

Place Names

Many of the place names in use at the time of first contact between the Native Americans of the Carolina coast and English settlers have changed dramatically over the centuries. Below are some examples of names used by local tribes or by the Europeans who lived alongside them, with their present-day counterparts.

Ittywan Island	Daniel Island
Mawan	alternative name for Daniel Island
Ittywan or Etiwan River	Cooper River
Wando River	original name of Cooper River
Watroo, Waticoe, Watcow	East Beresford Creek
Ittchicaw	West Beresford Creek
Kiawah River	Ashley River

The oldest surviving land grant for Daniel Island is dated January 1, 1675, and is held in the South Carolina State Archives in Columbia. It reads in part, "John Lord Berkeley Palatine and the rest of the Lords Palatine and proprietors of the Province of Carolina do hereby grant John Norton, Joiner, and Originall Jackson, Carpenter, a plantation of 400 acres of land English measure now in the possession of said John Norton and Originall Jackson situate and located upon Ittiwan Island." A plat, or scale drawing of the property, was attached to the grant, but like nearly all plats created before 1732, it has not survived. (Courtesy South Carolina State Archieves.)

2. Setting up the Carolina Colony

England first laid claim to an area called Carolina in 1629 when King Charles I granted Sir Robert Heath control over all the territory in North America between 31 degrees and 36 degrees north latitude (the land between Virginia and Florida) and stretching from ocean to ocean. Heath did not establish successful colonies and had to abandon his claim on Carolina with the execution of the king and the outbreak of the English Civil War, which lasted from 1642 to 1651. Shortly after the restoration of the monarchy in 1660, Charles II granted the same lands in March 1663 to a group of eight noblemen who had supported his return to the monarchy. The colony was to be a privately owned venture controlled by the eight Lords Proprietors: Edward, the Earl of Clarendon; George, the Duke of Albemarle; Lord Craven; Lord Berkeley; Lord Ashley Cooper; Sir George Carteret; Sir William Berkeley; and Sir John Colleton.

Early attempts by the Lords Proprietors to establish colonies in Carolina were limited to encouraging freemen who lived in Barbados and Bermuda to establish settlements in return for grants of land and promises of wealth from the commodities they could grow and sell. Initial reports from early explorations along the coast of Carolina promised wonderful weather and rich land that would support crops of ginger, tobacco, sugar, cotton, indigo, and oranges, as well as mulberry plants, essential in the raising of silkworms. A few attempts, including one at Cape Fear, ended in failure. It is possible that the national crises that confronted the English during this time also distracted the Lords Proprietors from fully focusing on their grant. The Great Plague hit London in 1665, and the next year the Great Fire destroyed a large part of the city. The English were also at war with the Dutch from 1665 to 1667.

First Arrivals

In 1669, Lord Ashley reinvigorated efforts to colonize Carolina. The grant from Charles II was not unlimited, and without progress, the

Pierre Mortier's 1696 map shows that Jacksons, Codner, Daniell, Norton, Morgan, and Friez had all built homes or established a plantation complex on the island by that time. Archeological investigations over the past decade have located the probable sites of these plantations. All have been declared potentially eligible for designation as national historic places and additional archeological investigations will take place before development can occur. (Courtesy Harry Frank Guggenheim Foundation.)

Crown would take back its charter and issue it to men who could develop the land and enrich England. Colonies to the north were flourishing in Virginia, Pennsylvania, New Jersey, and New York, and the lack of additional lands to exploit in Barbados and Bermuda made the lack of colonization in Carolina problematic for the proprietors. During a meeting of the Proprietors on April 26, 1669, each agreed to contribute £500 to purchase ships and equipment to establish a colony at Port Royal. It was also decided that a certain number of settlers would leave from England, with additional colonists to join the expedition in Ireland, Barbados, and Bermuda before arriving in Carolina. Incentives for these first settlers included guaranteed land grants, with the amount of land depending on the number of members of a family, including servants, who would make the journey, as well as promises of wealth from a percentage of the profits derived from crops produced on their lands

Lord Ashley also added one additional incentive. His experiences with the religious turmoil in 17th-century England had convinced him that promises of an ability to worship free of the fear of persecution was an important and highly attractive motivator that would bring people to his new colony. He was largely responsible for drafting the first constitutions for the government of Carolina, the Fundamental Constitutions, dated July 21, 1669, with 16 of the original 111 articles dealing with these guarantees of religious freedom. The noted philosopher John Locke is often credited with the creation of these articles, but at that time he had not yet begun the work that would make him famous. In the late 1660s and early 1670s, Locke was in fact the recording secretary for the Lords Proprietors, and he was paid £4 to record the articles.

The Fundamental Constitutions also established the eight Lords Proprietors as a Palatine Court, which was the basis of a hereditary nobility in Carolina.

Daniel Island lies in what was known as the Parish of St. Thomas and St. Denis. This dual name reflected the merger of two of the original 10 parishes of the Carolina colony established by the Church Act of 1706. The primary purpose of the act was to help in the governance of the colony, following a practice established in Barbados. In 1706, over 100 French Huguenots lived in St. Thomas Parish, and so the South Carolina Assembly established St. Denis Parish, named after the patron saint of France, so the French-speaking settlers could worship in their native language. It was intended that St. Denis would eventually merge with St. Thomas Parish when its people could understand English. The two parishes coexisted until 1768, when the Assembly dissolved St. Denis Parish and gave its assets to St. Thomas for the benefit of the poor. By the mid-1800s, parish names were rarely used to refer to locations. Instead the more commonly known judicial provinces, or districts, established in 1769, became the accepted names of locations. The Charleston District remained intact until portions were split off in 1800 to form Colleton County and again in 1882 to form Berkeley County.

Richard Codner was granted 76 acres on Daniel Island in 1680 and he and his heirs maintained an active settlement until the late 18th century. This site was uncovered during initial archeological explorations of what is believed to be the central complex of a plantation. Additional investigations are anticipated before the site is approved for full development.

Two classes of nobility were also established that would provide entitlement to large tracts of land that could then be sold to other future settlers. Landgraves were entitled to 48,000 acres, and caciques were entitled to 12,000 acres.

While the constitution was being drafted, Lord Ashley was also busy procuring the ships, equipment, and supplies that would transport and support these early settlers. It was well understood that food and supplies would have to be provided until enough land could be cleared to allow the planting of subsistence crops. Detailed lists of what was purchased have survived and include food, seeds, tools, clothing, small arms and cannon, and shot and powder. There was also £50 alloted for items to trade with the Native Americans, including beads, hats, hoes, axes, knives, and suits. It was fully expected that the lands they were intending to colonize were to be purchased from the Native Americans, and the South Carolina State Archives contain nearly half a dozen documents that detail the transfer of ownership of Lowcountry land from various tribes to the first caciques in Carolina.

Three ships were procured. The largest was a 300-ton frigate named *Carolina* obtained at a cost of £430. An additional £480 was spent on repairs and fitting out the vessel with new lines, sails, and the stores needed to support the crew of 17 men. The *Port Royal*, a frigate of 30 tons and a crew of seven, cost £125 and an additional £75 for repairs and stores. The third ship, the 20-ton shallop *Albemarle*, was crewed by five and cost £82 to purchase and equip. This fleet was under the command of Joseph West, who was chosen by the Lords Proprietors in a meeting on July 29, 1669. It was also at this meeting that they accepted the Fundamental Constitutions as drafted by Lord Ashley.

On August 17, the three ships departed Plymouth bound for Kinsail, Ireland with 92 family members and servants aboard the *Carolina* and five more aboard the *Port Royal*. The fleet arrived on August 30, and after taking on a few additional servants, sailed for Barbados on September 17, having been forced to wait for favorable winds. All three ships reached Barbados in late October. On November 2, a strong storm parted the anchor cables of the *Albemarle*, which ran aground on a rocky shore and was destroyed. A replacement ship, the *Three Brothers*, was found and hired.

Captain West and his ships sailed again in early November. While sailing through the Bahamas, another strong gale struck and scattered the fleet. The *Port Royal* ran aground near the island of Abaco and was damaged beyond repair. The *Three Brothers* fled north and in January 1670 reached Nansemond, a settlement in Virginia, where it reprovisioned and repaired damages sustained in the storm. The *Carolina* made it to Bermuda in early February but suffered severe damage to its stern that caused a great deal of

Left: *A typical colonial lock mechanism recovered from the Codner plantation site.* Right: *Part of an iron used to press clothing also recovered from the Codner plantation.*

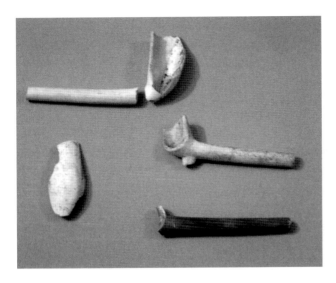

A vein of clay running through Daniel Island toward the town of Cainhoy contains a high percentage of kaolin. In the 17th and 18th centuries, kaolin was highly prized for the manufacture of the finest china. It was also used to make tobacco pipes such as the ones pictured here, recovered from the Codner plantation. Decorative molding was added after the 1730s.

flooding and the loss of most of the gunpowder in its hold. Captain West procured an additional ship in Bermuda, a sloop called the *Peggy*.

The *Carolina* left Bermuda on February 26 and arrived at Port Royal, near present-day Beaufort, on March 21. Captain West found the anchorage there to be very exposed to weather from the east, and no natural area that would allow for good defense from attacks by the Spanish, which was a constant concern for him. The local Native Americans who had met them told them about a place called Kiawah that would be much better suited for them. They set sail and arrived at Bulls Bay in late March and a few days later sailed to a high bluff on the Ashley River at the recommendation of the Kiawah Indians. There they established the town of Albemarle at the present location of Charlestowne Landing. The *Three Brothers* arrived from Virginia on May 23.

First Land Grants

Determining who Daniel Island's first European owners were is challenging for several reasons. First, much of the paper that was provided to record acts and land grants was destroyed aboard the *Carolina* in the gale off Bermuda, making record keeping a challenge. Also, the first surveyor-general attached to the colony, Florence O'Sullivan (whom Sullivan's Island is named after), was described by Henry Brayme in late 1670 as a "dissentious and ill tempered man who knew nothing about the craft of surveying" whose efforts at defining the boundaries of grants were inaccurate and often very late. It is also apparent when reading the early minutes of the colony's council meetings that disputes arose as to who was to be given land upon arrival, and how much. The most significant impediment to research, however, occurred over 80 years after these first settlements, when two hurricanes struck the city within 15 days of each other in 1752. The first, on September 15, was accompanied by a 17-foot storm surge that caused great damage and was accompanied by a large loss of life. The official records of the colony were held in a building that had up to three feet of standing water in it. Records from 1730 and later were recovered and dried out, but the original written land grants and records of conveyance, along with the plats, or drawings of land ownership, were lost. An incomplete collection of grant abstracts, now housed in the South Carolina State Archives, was created in the 1740s and remains a primary source of information on the early land transactions of the colony.

In 1675, a renewed attempt was made to standardize the process of granting land and consolidating the records of grants already made to the first settlers. Grants in 1674 and 1675 generally recognize that the "lands were already held." The case of one of the earliest recorded grants illustrates this. Originall Jackson, a carpenter, and John Norton, a joiner, arrived in the colony from Barbados in September 1670, having sailed on the *Carolina*. They formed a partnership and cleared land and planted together on Ittiwan Island until 1673. Their use of this land appears to have been somewhat controversial, as the governing council minutes from August 25, 1671 records the penalties they would incur if they did not formally receive a grant or warrant for the lands they were utilizing. This debate seems to have not been fully resolved until a grant was finally issued, which was in fact the second grant recorded by the Province of Carolina (the first was for a lot in the Town of Charlestown).

A year later, in late January 1676, 210 acres on "Etiwan Island" were granted to William Jones (these lands would be sold to Richard Codner a few years later); and 810 acres were granted to William Thomas, also on Etiwan Island. This made Thomas the largest landowner on present-day Daniel Island and it is surmised that some of his grant was for present-day Thomas Island. For a time, both islands were known as Thomas Island. Later that year, Mathew English and John Morgan were granted 140 acres on the island.

In May 1786, Joseph Atkinson filed a claim for 75 acres of marsh along the Cooper River just south of Scotts Ferry and adjoining land that he had purchased. This claim was not granted. Title to land in the 18th century was often disputed, especially during the time of new government procedures following the Revolutionary War. (Courtesy South Carolina State Archives.)

More land was granted within the colony over time, primarily along the Cooper and Ashley Rivers. The next grant on Daniel Island came on August 11, 1677, when William Jackson was granted 70 acres on the southern end of the island, and Richard Codner received a grant for 76 acres on lands "bounded to the west by Ittchecaw Creek," which was the Native American name for the western branch of Beresford Creek. James Hutton was granted 70 acres on Etiwan Island six days later. By 1733, this land would belong to Charles King.

On September 9, 1696, Robert Daniell was given a grant of 972 acres on Etiwan Island by the Lords Proprietors, for which he paid £20 per thousand acres. This gave him ownership of all remaining ungranted land on the island, with property bounded on the north by the lands of Ralph Wilson and to the west by the lands of Richard Codner. By 1715, records indicate that the island was starting to be named after Daniell. Over time, it changed on documents, maps, and charts from "Daniell" to "Daniels," and finally "Daniel."

It was at the time of Daniell's grant that the earliest map of the island was created. The 1696 map by Pierre Mortier titled "Carte Partiuleiere de la Caroline" shows eight landowners on the island, most traceable to the first holders of land grants. The eight were Richard Codner, Captain Robert William, Jackson Abot, John Norton, John Morgan, Iluetin (this may be James Hutton, who was granted 70 acres on August 17, 1677), and Cliffor (probably Elias Clifford, a mariner who was given a grant for 200 acres in 1692), and Captain Robert Daniell. A ninth grant appears to have been given to "Frize" for an island north of Ralston Creek, today called Roddin Island Two.

This portrait of Robert Daniell by Henrietta Johnston is believed to have been completed between 1708 and 1715. Johnston (1674–1729) was America's first female artist and first American artist to use pastels as a painting medium. Her family emigrated to England from northwestern France in 1687, and she began painting pastel portraits of Irish gentry in 1700. Her first husband, Robert Dering, died in 1702, and she emigrated to Carolina in 1708 with her second husband, the Reverend Gideon Johnston, rector of St. Philip's Episcopal Church in Charlestown. The Church of England was often slow to pay Reverend Johnston, and Henrietta supplemented their income with portraits of wealthy Charlestonians. (Courtesy Ken Daniel.)

3. Daniel Island's Early European Owners

While much of Daniel Island's history is told through the changing use of the land over time, there were at least three men, early landowners, who left indelible marks in the early days that would persist to the present. Robert Daniell, Isaac Lesesne, and Thomas Elfe came to the island from different backgrounds and contributed to its development in different ways, but taken together their stories show that they planted the seeds for all that was to come later.

Robert Daniell, Governor

The namesake of Daniel Island was to become a deputy proprietor of the Carolina colony and deputy governor of both North Carolina and South Carolina in his lifetime. A great deal of research has been done to trace his lineage by both historical societies and his heirs. The most complete research indicates that he was born in 1646 to John and Sarah Daniell in London. His father was a ship owner who held numerous properties in the London area. One of Robert's brothers, John Jr., was captain of the East India Company ship *New London*, which sailed between India, Java, and London. A letter-book of his survives and includes letters from John Jr. to Robert.

Robert was involved in the maritime trade between London, Barbados, and Bermuda, and the surviving records piece together the life of a London-based mariner who eventually made Carolina his home. A warrant, or order for land to be surveyed and granted, was issued to him in 1675 for land in the Carolina colony, but it appears not to have been executed. Also in that year, Robert Daniell II was born to Robert and his wife, Dorothy. Robert II married Sarah Proctor, whose father owned land across Beresford Creek just to the north of Daniel Island. They had two children, and he became a mariner as well. However, he was lost at sea sometime between October 20, 1709 and July 1, 1710. Little is known about Dorothy before Robert II's birth, nor is there a surviving record of their marriage. Dorothy died on October 16, 1711.

By 1677, Robert Daniell was listed as a "freeman" of the colony, which means that he had established residency there. He was issued a warrant for 500 acres,

Governor Robert Daniell died May 1, 1718, and was buried on his settlement. His church, St. Phillip's, had been badly damaged by a hurricane in 1710. Another hurricane in 1713 and the Yemasee Indian war of 1715 delayed reconstruction, and the church did not reopen until 1723. It is presumed that Daniell's remains were moved to St. Phillip's in downtown Charleston shortly after that. The original crypt stone was recovered in 1895 when a Mr. Tobias bought a vacant lot and began building on it. The stone was moved to the front of St. Phillip's, and in 1908 the Colonial Dames had this stone created, which is on the back wall of the church.

but again it does not appear to have been executed. On June 3, 1678, Daniell was granted a lot in the new town being laid out on nearby Oyster Point, the present-day location of Charleston, at the confluence of the Ashley and Cooper Rivers. He purchased additional lots there in 1681 and 1683.

Captain Daniell's growing wealth soon led him into the political arena. In 1680, he became part of the group of freemen who opposed Landgrave John Colleton, the Goose Creek Men, and his fortunes seem to have been placed on hold. This dispute centered on Colleton's effectiveness and on his decisions, and reflected tensions among the Lords Proprietors on the management of the colony. Lord Ashley, in a letter to Governor West and the rest of the Carolina Counsel, advised them "to keep unbiased the rules of the Fundamental Constitutions Temporary Laws and Instructions, and in particular to remember that deputies represent the persons of the Proprietors. . . . And not to submit to the will of any Governor or to Sir Colleton if they should attempt to influence or exert undue power when so much care had been made to ensure a sharing of power." Adding to the tension was the settlers' refusal to ratify the Fundamental Constitutions. The first draft, which had been approved by the Lords Proprietors in 1669, underwent a revision in March 1670 that added nine additional articles. Revisions three and four were written in 1682. All were rejected by the settlers, as they considered the constitutions to unfairly restrict their political and economic freedoms.

Two events in 1686 and 1688 changed Robert Daniell's life. The first was the invasion of the Port Royal River by three Spanish warships in August 1686. The Spanish had attempted to establish a colony there a decade earlier and viewed the land as Spanish territory. The English settlement of Stuart was located nearby, and it was quickly overrun by the Spanish. The invaders then attacked a second settlement called New London, or Willtown. The governor, James Colleton, sent Captain Daniell, who owned several ships, and 90 men to reinforce Major Boone's men, who had been sent south days earlier.

These 90 men were not part of a standing military force. Rather, they were called up or mobilized when the colony was threatened. It was a requirement that all "inhabitants and freemen of Carolina above 17 years of age and under 60 be bound to bear arms and serve as soldiers whenever the Grand Council shall find it necessary." Daniell was also able to gather up a sizable force of Native Americans who had promised support to the English and were willing to help defend them against the Spanish.

There is no record of Captain Daniell's forces actually engaging the Spanish. A hurricane struck the day after they arrived at Port Royal, on August 26, severely damaging Daniell's ships. This storm, in addition to the rapid deployment of Daniell and Boone, forced the Spanish to retreat back to St. Augustine. Some refer to this hurricane as the "Spanish Repulse" as it disrupted more aggressive Spanish plans to press their attack on the Carolina colony.

In 1688, the "glorious revolution" occurred in England when William III and Mary II overthrew King James II in a bloodless revolution (Charles II had died in 1685). Deeply tied to the continuing rift between Catholics and Protestants, this change of monarchs re-established the rule of the Anglican Church in England. It also greatly improved Daniell's political position, since he had sided with the pro-Anglican forces. Captain Daniell continued to ply his trade as a merchant trader and ship captain throughout the early 1690s. In November 1693, *The Daniell of Carolina* was severely damaged in a storm, probably while enroute to or from Barbados. Daniell also purchased another lot in the city in January 1694.

His first grant of land on Daniel Island came in 1695, when he acquired land along the Wando River during the tenure of John Archdale's governorship of the colony. This is where he would build "Daniell's Pier" and a settlement that employed a "considerable number of slaves." He also obtained the 62-acre island that is the present-day home of the Blackbaud complex, which was then named Brady Island or St. Jogues Island. Daniell sold St. Jogues to Richard Codner in 1715.

By early 1698, the Lords Proprietors had been unable to gain acceptance and ratification of the Fundamental Constitutions. Captain Daniell returned to London that year and with Edmond Bellinger was helping the Lords Proprietors to develop a fifth revision to the document. The work was completed by April, but it too was swiftly rejected by the colonists.

A significant change was made in 1698 to the manner in which landgraves and caciques could be granted. The nobility of Carolina was now available for purchase, with the title of landgrave available for £100 and cacique for £50. Daniel was made a landgrave without cost on August 18, 1698, and was also granted the right to sell six titles of landgrave and eight of cacique. This entitled him to 48,000 acres in Carolina, and his early acquisitions upon returning to the colony included all the unclaimed land on Daniell Island, Parris Island to the South, extensive lands along the Santee and a large estate just south of present-day Georgetown. Edmond Bellinger, who had acquired minor holdings in the colony on Hog Island (now the location of Patriots Point) and two small islands near Daniel Island on the Cooper, purchased a landgrave title. He later obtained significant amounts of land to the south and west of Charlestown.

In 1699, Captain Robert Daniell divorced Dorothy and married Martha Wainwright, a Charlestown native who was born in 1684 and was 16 years old at the time of the wedding. Their primary residence was believed to be in Charlestown, with Daniell's settlement on the island being a working plantation that likely produced products for export or for sale in Charlestown. He also continued working as a merchant captain and ship owner.

In September 1702, the Spanish again threatened the Carolinas and the expanding English settlements. Captain Daniell again responded to the threat, leading naval and ground forces in attacks against Spanish settlements in Florida. He was successful in taking St. John and St. Mary's and made several attacks against St. Augustine, but the Spanish were able to defeat him there primarily due to the lack of sufficient numbers of British ground troops and heavy cannon to support their attack.

In March 1703, Captain Daniell was appointed the deputy governor of North Carolina by Sir Nathaniel Johnson, and he and Martha moved to Archbell Point, North Carolina, where he bought a 270-acre plantation. They lived there until the middle of 1705, and his first two children were born there as well. Sarah was born on November 6, 1703, and Martha was born on December 2, 1704. His last two children by Martha were born in Charlestown: John, who was born on March 29, 1707, and Ann, born on April 15, 1710.

In 1711, an uprising of the Tuscarora Indians in North Carolina was incited by the French and Spanish, and Captain Daniell commanded a contingent of soldiers that successfully put an end to the hostilities. In recognition of his continued service to the proprietorship and to the cause of the crown, Queen Anne granted him another landgrave of 48,000 acres on January 22, 1713. Daniell once again took up arms in defense of English interests in the Yemassee War of 1715. Spanish and French agitation had continued since the earlier uprising and they were able to unite nearly all of the Native American tribes to revolt against the expanding presence of the English.

Daniell was appointed the 18th governor under proprietary rule on April 25, 1716, a post he held until April 30, 1717. He died on his plantation May 1, 1718 at the age of 72, and was originally interred on the island. At some point his remains were transferred to St. Phillip's church in the city. His grave marker was found in January 1895 in what appeared to be an abandoned lot across the street from the main graveyard. The stone had covered a well and was damaged by the well pipe and pump chain.

Isaac Lesesne, Huguenot

The foundation of the Carolina colony was based in part on a premise that freedom of political expression and religious worship were essential rights and

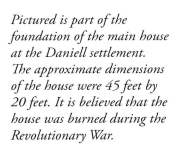

Pictured is part of the foundation of the main house at the Daniell settlement. The approximate dimensions of the house were 45 feet by 20 feet. It is believed that the house was burned during the Revolutionary War.

The fire that destroyed the main house of the Daniell settlement melted this wine bottle. Note the hand-applied lip on the bottle.

were to be guaranteed. This was extremely attractive to many Europeans at a time when English Catholics were being persecuted by the Church of England and French Protestants were being attacked for their beliefs in a predominately Catholic nation. In all nations the rules and privileges of the monarchy were impediments to the lower class's freedom and ability to improve their lives.

In 1680, the first 45 French settlers arrived in Carolina. They were Huguenots, or French Protestants, and over the next few years many more of them migrated as individuals and as families. In 1685, Louis XIV revoked the Edict of Nantes and the persecution of French Protestants greatly increased. Thousands fled France in the ensuing decades, and 326 chose Charlestown between 1680 and 1700.

Isaac Lesesne was one of these early migrants from France, and he obtained 171 acres of land on Daniel Island in 1699. He had come from a wealthy family in France, and quickly established a viable plantation in his new home. Lesesne married twice and fathered eight children, three by his first wife Elizabeth Tresvant: Isaac Jr., Henry, and Esther. His second wife Francis Netherton bore him five children: Daniel, Frances, Sarah, John, and Peter George. The eldest son, Isaac Lesesne Jr., took over the plantation in 1736 when his father died. The plantation, known as "The Grove," flourished under Isaac Lesesne Jr., with a shop opening up on Market Street in Charlestown to sell their goods. These goods included cotton, indigo, and meat from their extensive livestock including cattle, sheep, and hogs.

The Grove, like most Daniel Island plantations, was a producer of industrial goods as well. Naval stores, lime, and lumber were produced in great quantities there. In 1752, Lesesne contributed 5,312 bushels of lime toward the construction of St. Michael's church in Charlestown. The plantation was also providing yellow pine and oak planks for shipbuilding operations along the Wando at that time.

Lesesne married Elizabeth Walker and had seven children: Sarah, Isaac, Elizabeth, William, Daniel, Thomas, and Juliana. In 1767, he filed a memorial for 700 acres that traced its ownership to Governor Daniell. Upon Lesesne's death in 1772, the estate, now consisting of 988 acres, was divided between his three oldest sons. His eldest son Isaac Walker Lesesne received the northern portion, which retained the name The Grove. During the Revolutionary War, Isaac Walker served in the Continental army under Col. Peter Horry. His regiment was part of Francis Marion's brigade. In 1792, Isaac Walker Lesesne died and Hannah North was given ownership of the plantation. In 1808, the plantation was sold to Joshua Leavitt, ending 99 years of Lesesne ownership of The Grove.

Thomas Elfe, Cabinetmaker

Thomas Elfe owned the island that Blackbaud and Blackbaud Stadium are now built on. In the 18th century, he was Charlestown's most famous and successful cabinetmaker, and it is felt that the proportions and elegance of his work were unsurpassed in the colonies, even compared with Philadelphia cabinetmakers.

Elfe was born in London in 1719 and apprenticed under his uncle, who was a cabinetmaker there. He arrived in Virginia In 1740 and made his way

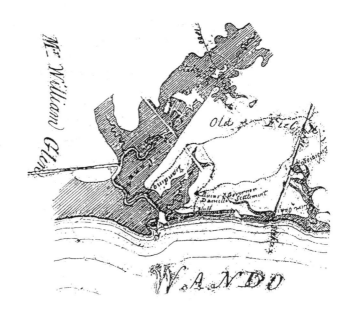

This 1786 plat of the Lesesne plantation shows (near center) the location of the Robert Daniell settlement on the Wando River with the annotation "Ruins of Governor Daniell's Settlement." (Courtesy Charleston County RMC and Brockington and Associates.)

37

Pictured is Daniell's Pier on the Wando River near the point where the 1784 plat shows a road terminating at the water's edge. The pier is made of palmetto logs with evident wood-peg construction, meaning that no nails were used.

within seven years to Charlestown, which at that time held outstanding opportunities for a producer of the highest quality furniture. Many of those who lived in the city and on the numerous nearby plantations had tremendous personal wealth, fueled by the largest port in colonial America and its agricultural products of rice, naval stores, and indigo as well as a rapidly developing shipbuilding industry.

Shortly after he arrived in Charlestown, Elfe married Mary Hancock, a widow, in 1748. He became a widower himself within the first year of marriage, but remarried in 1755 to Rachel Prideau. Elfe and his second wife had six children: William, Elizabeth, Hannah, George, Thomas, and Benjamin.

In 1765, Elfe purchased a 250-acre plantation from Benjamin Burnham that included St. Jogues Island, where the Blackbaud campus is located today. This was one of several land purchases he made around this time. Other wealthy Charlestown businessmen had plantations and were making money on both the agricultural and industrial products produced on them, as well as on the appreciation of the property.

The main plantation house was in about the same location as the Blackbaud office building today. A landing serving the plantation was near the present-day bridge over the smaller arm of Beresford Creek. Elfe improved the existing structures, including the addition of an extra chimney and fireplace, and interior plastering. The plantation produced fruit and seeds for the local market, cattle that were sold for meat, wool from a number of sheep, firewood, and, it is presumed, lumber for Elfe's cabinetmaking business in the city. He had a sailing barge that transported people and goods from the landing along Beresford Creek to the wharves of Charlestown.

Elfe's home was downtown and his shop was located at 54 Queen Street, where today there is an establishment called the Thomas Elfe Workshop. By the 1760s, he was producing an average of 17 to 30 pieces a year and his net worth at the time of his death would have made him a multi-millionaire in today's dollars. Some of his work is on display at the Charleston Museum.

Thomas Elfe died at the end of 1775, at a time when his position as a staunch Loyalist was beginning to adversely affect his business. His wife Rachel moved to the plantation sometime before 1780 and continued to produce agricultural products for sale in the city. Even there she did not escape persecution for her Loyalist support, for on September 24, 1781, a year or so after the British had occupied Charlestown, a Colonial raiding party plundered the plantation, breaking down fences and turning her horses into the cornfield.

Rachel Elfe died in January 1805, and one of their sons, George, inherited the plantation. Records indicate he continued to work the plantation in a manner similar to his father, employing up to 28 slaves to manage and produce the crops and tend to the cows and sheep on the island. By the mid-1820s however, the Charleston economy was not strong. In 1826, three years before his death, George Elfe sold the plantation to John E. Farr for $3,500.

A significant complex was built on the small island just north of Daniell's settlement that included a large wharf and possibly a warehouse, plus a central cooking or food preparation area that may have been for the slaves and freemen who worked on the site. This foundation is believed to have been related to the kitchen fireplaces. Historical reclamation has been completed at this site and it is expected that homes will be built there.

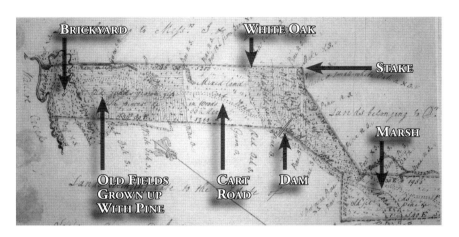

This 1797 plat of land belonging to the estate of Anne Delahow was drafted by Joseph Purcell, a surveyor who did a great deal of work on Daniel Island after the Revolutionary War. Surveyors used trees and drainage ditches to mark property lines, and placed stakes when needed. The plats they produced also showed how the land was being used at the time, and by the late 1790s, much of Daniel Island had reverted to unused fields that were returning to mixed pine and hardwood forest, reflecting the hardships the war had placed on Daniel Island's owners. The Delahow brickyard and associated cart roads are also marked, along with a dam used to contain the marsh to the southeast and keep the land to the north dry enough for use as pasture. (Courtesy Charleston County RMC.)

4. Colonial Agriculture and Industry

The Carolina colony was formed as a private enterprise with objectives of both settling the new American territories under the English crown and making money for the eight Lords Proprietors. Glowing reports from the first explorers of the Carolina coast promised weather similar to Barbados and soils rich and fertile. The first few years were spent trying to grow the same crops that prospered on Barbados: cotton, indigo, tobacco, ginger, oranges, and mulberry. But the frosts came early and often during the first several winters, and after five years, the Lords Proprietors were anxious to start getting a return on their investments. Timber products became the colony's first exports, and by the early 1700s, there was also significant trade in fur and animal pelts, especially deer, as well as in naval stores and rice.

Daniel Island was well situated to be a significant part of these first agricultural and industrial endeavors. Navigable water bounded the island to the east and west, large stands of oak and pine grew abundantly in the fertile soil on the highlands, and clay suitable for the manufacture of bricks provided the island's owners a means to seek their riches from the products of the land.

Timber

The island's forests were the first resource to be exploited. The large straight poles that could be used for the masts and other spars of sailing ships were among the first products exported from Charlestown to Barbados and England as early as 1672. Live oak and yellow pine were also immediately valuable to the building of the city and its local industries. The oaks that were not used in building provided a local source of firewood and are commonly seen on the production registers of the Daniel Island plantations. An advertisement for the Elfe plantation in 1805 noted that the landing was capable of handling boats with 15 cords of firewood. All heating in the colonial Lowcountry was by firewood and sources that could be easily shipped to the city by water were most desireable. Isaac Lesesne also had several sawmills on his property and supplied timber to the local shipbuilding industries both on Daniel Island and at Hobcaw, home of the south's largest shipyards.

Left: *This heavy iron felling ax was used to cut timber for markets and to clear land for agriculture. It dates from the 18th century and was recovered from the Codner Plantation site.* Right: *Craftsmen who shaped wood for buildings, ships, or farm implements used an adze like this. A wooden handle would have been fitted through the hole, and a hammer used to either cut into the wood or shave off layers depending upon the needs of the craftsman.*

Naval Stores

The colonial landowners of Daniel Island were very familiar with the term naval stores, which referred to the resin, tar, cordage, and pitch that sailing vessels required for their building and upkeep. Lord Ashley sent a jar of naval tar to England in 1674 to see if the admiralty was interested in the type of tar and pitch that could be produced by the colony. The long leaf southern pine and yellow pine that dominated Daniel Island in the late 1600s and early 1700s were excellent sources for these products, and archeological research on the island has confirmed that naval stores were produced and shipped from here.

At the turn of the 18th century, Britain encouraged the American colonies to produce naval stores. Russia's invasion of Sweden and Finland had cut off the traditional British source of pine tar and pitch, and the rich stands of pine in the Carolina colony were seen as a way to replace them. In 1705, the Bounty Act placed a premium on tar and resin exported to England. By 1725, when the bounty was rescinded, four-fifths of the tar and pitch used by England was produced in the southern American colonies and shipped primarily through Charlestown.

Pine tar is derived from the roots and stumps of dead pine trees, which are rich in resin. This lightwood was collected and placed in a circular pit lined with clay and allowed to burn slowly. The heat liquefied the resin, which was collected at the bottom of the pit and put into barrels. This pine tar was used on ships to preserve exposed wood and rigging. A denser product, called pitch, could be obtained by heating the pine tar and driving off much of its water. Cotton cord, when soaked in pitch, was used to fill the seams between the planks of a ship's hull, making it watertight.

Two pits were uncovered during archeological investigations near the Family Circle Cup complex that were determined to be similar to those associated with the production of tar. These pits were lined with clay fragments and have a tube or neck of thick clay that would have collected the tar as the wood was heated. They were estimated to have been in use sometime before 1740. There are also two larger circular pits on Bellinger Island that are of the proper size and arrangement to have been used to produce pine tar.

Brick Making

The soil conditions and geography of Daniel Island were not ideal for the production of stable agricultural crops such as rice. However, the island's early owners found a very profitable use for the clay that dominates most of the Wando basin when they turned to the manufacture of bricks. Brick making has been an established art since the days of early Egyptian civilization, and many of the early Charlestown settlers brought with them the knowledge and skills to make bricks of sufficient durability and hardness to be used as building materials.

As early as 1664, correspondence from the colony noted that there was good clay in the area for making bricks, but that it was grayer than what had

Most agricultural tools were made of iron, such as this rice hoe, and were imported into the colony from England. They were of various sizes and shapes. The triangular sliver of iron was driven into the collar after a wooden handle had been fitted, to lock the handle into place.

The Delahow brickyard today shows evidence of shell middens and the borrow pits from which the clay was mined. After completion of archeological recovery activities, this site became the location of the kayak launch pier.

been used before. In 1682, it was noted that "excellent brick was being made in Charlestown, but just not much of it." Then in 1713 a fire destroyed a large part of the city, which had been mostly built of wood. The assembly passed an act that required all buildings be made of brick, but it was repealed in 1715 as not enough brick was available to support the growth of the city. In 1740, building codes were again modified to require brick construction following another fire in November of that year.

Daniel Island's clay possesses good qualties for brick making, and it is found in abundance on the island. In addition to a ready supply of the proper kinds of clay, Daniel Island also provided other elements needed for the production of bricks, including a cheap but skilled labor force, water, sand, firewood, and transportation to a market.

Brick making was done in the agricultural off season with a limited number of highly specialized workers. Clay was dug by hand from shallow pits, called borrow pits, which were a distinctive feature of brick making before the Civil War and that survive in many places today. Aerial photographs reveal many borrow pits, which from the ground appear as large circular freshwater ponds. After the clay was dug from the pits, it was stored in heaps several feet high over the winter months, which weathered, or matured, the clay. Sand and water were added to improve the clay's working characteristics. The mixing of the materials was done by hand or by animals driving a paddle or wheel. Lime was often added as well to help melt the grains of sand and cause them to bind together in the fired brick. When the clay was properly mixed, it was forced into hardwood molds. The cabinetmaker Thomas Elfe manufactured these out of mahogany.

After molding, the bricks were allowed to dry for two to three weeks in open shelters that protected them from rain and direct sun. Once dry they were fired in kilns for two to ten days to harden the clay into a suitable building brick. The bricks would take several more weeks to cool before they could be removed and used. Most brick kilns were not permanent, but rather were built near a source of clay while brick making was in progress.

An expert brickmaker could make between 3,000 and 5,000 bricks per day, and a team could make up to 9,000. The cost of bricks was $4 to $7 per thousand from the Revolutionary War to the Civil War.

On Daniel Island, seven distinct sizes of bricks have been found. Until the late 1800s there was little standardization of bricks, which were generally made in whatever size suited the needs of the builder. On some large projects, including the city wall of Charlestown, builders specified one size since the bricks were supplied by many different brick makers.

Tidal Mills

Historically, many Carolina mill towns grew up around the fall line, where the rapid change in elevation from the piedmont to the coastal plains created small waterfalls and rapid streams. Columbia, Charlotte, and Spartanburg are examples of Carolina towns where this source of energy was tapped to

The clay found throughout the Wando Basin is ideal for making bricks. Until the Santee River was diverted to the Cooper in the 1940s, the Cooper River would often dwindle to a small stream, especially in the drier winter months. This 1949 aerial photograph of the Cooper River and Daniel Island shows three borrow pits now in the river, where clay was mined to be made into bricks. Typically, the gathering of clay was a winter chore when the need for labor in the fields was minimal. (Courtesy USDA.)

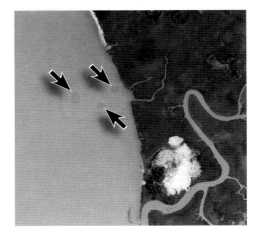

Aerial photography often reveals the location of borrow pits. Circular formations that were once dug out to a depth of 5 to 10 feet to obtain the proper clay for brick making gradually became freshwater marshes, many of which remain today (indicated by black arrows). The Scotts Ferry Road, also evident in this 1949 picture, ended at a protected area between several small islands still present today on the Cooper River. (Courtesy U.S. Department of Agriculture.)

power grist mills that ground wheat and corn into flour, and sawmills that cut lumber for the rapidly growing towns. Charlestown, however, had few rapidly flowing rivers and many small streams that would dry up completely in the summer. But it did have another source of water power in the tides, especially during the new and full moons, when the difference between high and low tide is almost seven feet.

Tidal mills have been used in Europe and England since the 9th century, and several working tidal mills are still maintained in England. An enclosed pond is built with a gate so that water can flow in as the tide rises and be trapped at high tide when the gate is shut. After the tide ebbs, the difference in water height can be used to power a water wheel to grind grain or cut lumber.

The large "free" labor pool that slavery provided until the Civil War was the primary means of grinding grain or cutting lumber for the growing shipbuilding industry across the Hobcaw River and the building of homes and offices in the Charleston area. In 1784, John Lucus, a native of northern England and the son of a tidal mill owner, was shipwrecked just to the north of Charleston. His observations of the laborious and inefficient manner of de-husking rice before it was shipped to England motivated him to build the first water-powered mill in South Carolina on Shem Creek. He continued to build stream-powered and tidal-powered mills into the early 1800s, and after his death his son continued to build mills, incorporating steam engines in the early 1840s.

Landowners on Daniel Island no doubt saw an opportunity to take advantage of previously unusable saltwater marshes and increase the efficiency of their lumbering operations. Much of the island at this time was still heavily forested with long leaf pine as well as oak and other hardwoods, all in high demand by the shipbuilding industry. Mills also gave them the ability to provide a for-profit service grinding the rice grown upstream on the Wando and Cooper Rivers.

Mills built along tidal creeks in the south were primarily made of wood. Due to their proximity to the ocean and the hurricanes that frequent the southeast, none have survived intact. However, there is ample evidence in the newspapers of the time that mills were in operation on Daniel Island. Knowing the mills' specific requirements helps to identify their locations today. They had to be near a river or stream with full flow at high and low tides, there had to be enough marshland for a pond of sufficient volume to power a waterwheel, and they had to be near roads or paths that would allow transportation of raw and finished goods to and from the mill.

Three tidal mill locations have been found on Daniel Island, including the surviving foundation timbers of one on the Wando River near a small tidal stream almost directly east of the Pierce Park Pool. The second is around Bellinger

Large piles of broken brick along a river or creek, like this brick-fall near the Daniell plantation house, are a classic indicator of a brick kiln site. Erosion of the banks of the Wando has exposed a growing expanse of brick that is particularly impressive at very low tides. The nearby pier structures, also visible at low tide, would have allowed the bricks to be loaded for shipment.

Left: *The first brick-making operations were done primarily by hand. A large demand for bricks, along with competitive pricing, led many plantation owners to employ mechanical devices to mix the clay and form the bricks. These first devices were often poor performers when it came to the thorough mixing of clay and sand, a vital step in the bricks' final, fired strength.* Right: *This is a product of early automated brick making. Clay was forced through an extrudor, and a knife or wire was used to cut the bricks to the proper size. If the mix was too dry, or forced through too fast, "scalloping" occurred along the edges, much like what happens when Play-Doh is forced through its machine too quickly.*

Island near the path between the boat parking lot and the island. Remnants of the dikes used to contain the water can be seen in satellite photographs. The third is near the ruins of Governor Daniell's house, where archeologists believe the marsh to the west would have contained the millpond.

Lime Kilns

Lime was an important industrial product in the colonial era. It was used in limited amounts in the manufacture of bricks, in the making of tabby, or cement that used shells as an aggregate, and in the plaster that covered the inside walls of wealthier families' homes.

Lime is relatively simple to produce but very labor intensive. Materials for the making of lime, and the slave labor force, were in ready supply on Daniel

Island. Numerous shell middens were left by Native Americans from their time on the island, and these, as well as additional oyster shells continually harvested from the local waters, provided a source for the necessary calcium carbonate. Coral and limestone have also been found along the banks of the Wando, and these raw materials could have been a supplement for oysters in the manufacture of lime. The final component, a ready source of oak firewood, was provided by the active live oak harvesting industry that supplied the nearby shipyards.

The oyster shells were burned in hot oak fires, where temperatures reached 2,000 degrees Fahrenheit. The resulting chemical process released carbon dioxide and left behind pure calcium oxide. After the fire cooled, the lime was harvested for sale or for use on the plantation. A typical firing could produce 200 or 300 bushels.

A lime kiln was found on the Lesesne plantation during archeological research in 1985. There is also a record of Thomas Elfe purchasing lime from Isaac Lesesne in April and October 1770 at a cost of a little over £5 for 55 bushels. Each bushel of lime could produce up to six bushels of lime mortar or up to four bushels of lime plaster.

Lime mortar was used to join the brickwork in a masonry structure. Lime, when mixed with sand, forms a joint that is weather tight and that binds the bricks together. Courser sand was used for areas that would be out of plain sight, while a finer sand was used for exterior and final course work.

Left: *The traditional red color of bricks is due to the presence of iron oxide in the clay. An unusually high firing temperature will change the iron oxide into black oxide, which produces a darker blue color. The bricks that were closest to the hardwood fires were often "over fired," as seen in this brick.*

Lime was used to make a plaster for interior walls. A wooden lattice was built over a home's interior walls, and the plaster applied in two to three coats. Plaster found on the island shows a two-layer construction (upper left) that was painted a dark green after it had dried (upper right). Imprints from the supporting lattice can be seen on the back of the fragments (bottom).

The lime was also used to make a cement tabby, which can be seen in many old buildings and foundations. Instead of sand, broken shells were used as a filler or aggregate.

Another use of lime was for plastering the interior walls of houses. Unlike the gypsum-based drywall that was introduced in the early 1900s and is still used in modern-day construction, the lime-based plaster hardened into a cement-like covering. Two to three coats were usually applied to a wall, with the final coat being a very fine white lime that could then be painted or papered.

Ship Building

In the early 19th century, there was a need for the young United States to maintain a fleet of naval vessels to ensure that its commerce and interests could be protected. A large fleet of powerful warships would have possibly been seen as a challenge to British domination of the world's oceans, so President Thomas Jefferson instead decided to commission 10 smaller gunboats. These ships were to be about 70 feet long, and carry two 32-pound cannons. The prototypes were built at the Washington Navy Yard, and contracts were then let for the remaining eight to be built in shipyards along the coast. Locally, Paul Pritchard was an acclaimed shipbuilder known for sturdy, seaworthy vessels. He completed the *John Adams* in his Hobcaw Creek shipyard in 1799, and undertook the building of "Gun Boat No. 9" at his Fair Bank Plantation shipyard on Daniel Island.

Gun Boat No. 9 was launched in March 1803 and, according to the U.S. Navy, was constructed of "the stoutest and best materials in her frame. . . . And is the very best boat on every account for carrying guns and for safety at sea." Shortly after her launch, she sailed to the Mediterranean Sea with Gun Boat No. 2, a journey of 27 days, and joined seven other gunboats in support of other U.S. ships in protecting American shipping, especially along the Barbary Coast. The flotilla returned to Charleston in the middle of 1806 as a result of the reduction in the size of the Mediterranean Fleet. It is believed that Prichard continued to produce small ships and coastal craft at his plantation until his death in 1814.

Daniel Island's only other known shipyard was operated by Richard Fordham on Moonham Plantation, located on present-day Ralston Creek. It is thought that Fordham's watercraft were used in local and coastal trade. In addition to warships, there was a need for ships and barges of all types to carry the produce from upriver plantations down to Charleston for further shipment to other ports around the world. Local commerce was chiefly

Pictured is tabby cement from the Lesesne Cemetery

The foundation timbers of a tidal mill along the Wando River have started to erode out of the bank. High ground on either side of the stream contains broken bricks and cobblestones and provided a hard, stable platform for the products to be sent to and from the mill. Remnants of a pier just south of this mill would have supported the loading of grain or rice.

carried in barrels, and ship builders often advertised a vessel's capacity in this way. John Daniell, no relation to Governor Daniell, was building and selling large deck barges in 1739 that were "capable of carrying 150 barrels of rice." Archeological research at Moonham plantation has found woodworking tools and other evidence of an active shipyard that existed in the early 1800s.

Rice

Charlestown became a center of wealth and trade in the early 18th century thanks largely to rice, and the legacy of this crop is still evident in travels up the Ashley and Cooper Rivers. Rice was grown on Daniel Island, but in quantities that were not significant when compared with the rice trade coming down the rivers from the larger plantations. "Wet rice" was the preferred crop, grown in large fields that were kept underwater by means of gates that allowed river water to flood the land in a controlled fashion. However, the water has to be fresh, not saltwater. Daniel Island is not far enough upriver to have enough freshwater to support the growing of wet rice. Dry rice agriculture was practiced on the island, but it is doubtful that it was a significant focus for the early landowners. Yields were significantly lower per acre than what could be achieved upriver, and the crops required significantly more labor to cultivate on a barrel-by-barrel comparison.

Indigo

This bushy plant produces a deep royal-blue dye that was highly sought after by European traders. Indigo seeds were brought to the Carolina colony early in its history, but the highly successful cultivation of rice in the early 18th century removed much of the incentive to grow any other crop. By the mid-1700s however, wildly fluctuating prices for rice motivated plantation owners to diversify their agricultural products. In 1740, the 17-year-old Elizabeth Lucas was sent indigo seeds from Barbados by her father, who had left her in charge of his Carolina plantation while he traveled to his other holdings in the West Indies. Early attempts to grow the plants failed, as they were not reaching maturity before the fall growing season ended. Lucas finally found that a very early spring planting allowed time for the bush to produce leaves that by June were full of the juices needed to make the dye.

Lucas also perfected the method to extract the dye from the plants. First they were soaked in water in a large tub, and when it had turned a deep yellow, the water was drained into a second vat, where several hours of beating caused blue flakes to appear. When the water was a light green, lime

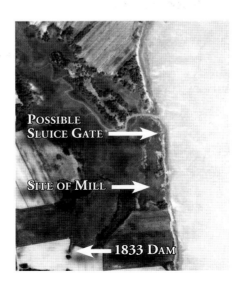

This 1949 aerial survey of Daniel Island shows the remnants of the millpond that supported the Wando tidal mill. (Courtesy U.S. Department of Agriculture.)

These shipbuilding tools were recovered from the Fordham's Moonsham plantation. (Courtesy Brockington and Associtates.)

was added to the vat and the flakes settled to the bottom. This produced a muddy, dark blue paste, which was allowed to dry and then sold as dye. In 1748, at the urging of the Charlestown merchant Henry Laurens, an act of parliament established a bounty of six pence per pound of indigo. By 1754, 217,000 pounds of indigo were exported from Charlestown, and just before the Revolutionary War, 1.2 million pounds were being exported every year.

Sea Island Cotton

Daniel Island, although not necessarily considered a sea island, was nonetheless an ideal environment for growing *Gossypium barbadense*, commonly called creole cotton or sea island cotton. Significant quantities of sea island cotton were produced on Daniel Island from the late 1700s until the early 1900s.

Sea island cotton is native to the Andes of South America and was imported to the Lowcountry in 1790 from Barbados. It differs significantly from the upland cotton grown further inland. Its fibers are much longer than common cotton and allow the weaving of luxurious material with a finer weave.

The sea island cotton plant requires a highly humid, salty environment to flourish, and is very susceptible to hard freezes. The tides around Daniel Island that keep the water salty and unusable for wet rice farming provided ideal conditions for sea island cotton. Dr. John B. Irving, in his 1842 book *A Day on the Cooper River*, noted that the land on Daniel Island was "valuable, and produces excellent Sea-Island Cotton." In 1850, 85 percent of the cotton grown in St. Thomas and St. Denis Parish was grown on Daniel Island, and in 1860, the production on Daniel Island exceeded all Charleston-area sea islands except Edisto.

The Civil War devastated the southern cotton industry, which had depended upon the labor of its slave population. However, cotton remained a viable crop on the island and landowners continued to produce sea island cotton into the late 1800s. Records from the Cunningham estate in 1903 show that 1,146 pounds of ginned cotton sold for $220.22. Cotton production continued on the lower 3,000 acres of Daniel Island until 1905, when the land was sold to A. F. Young and converted into a truck farm that planted asparagus, cabbage, cucumbers, potatoes, and beans. Cotton production on the northern 1,000 acres, the Furman Track, stopped around 1919 due to infestations of the boll weevil, which destroyed upwards of 90 percent of the sea island cotton crop in the Lowcountry.

Sailing ships required heavy weights for stability, like these ballast stones along the Wando near Prichard's shipyard. Typically, ballast was in the form of dense, round stones from European or Caribbean river beds. Shipowners preferred the rounded river stones because they minimized damage to the inside of the hull. Ships with little or no cargo took on stones as temporary ballast, and dumped them when they took on loads in Charleston. The stones left behind were valuable building material for roads and foundations.

In 1792, Joseph Purcell drafted this plat to show "the shape and body of land called Hartford complied of diverse tracts. Containing in the whole two thousand, three hundred and sixty one acres with 1007 acres of high land, cleared and in woods and 494 acres of marsh lands some parts improved. Belonging to Isaac Parker Esq." Notable features include the public road established in 1712 between the estate of George Smith and Daniel Island, and the location of the Hanford settlement, where Harry Guggenheim built his Cain Hoy lodge in 1934. The plat also contains details of the original land grants from the Lords Proprietors, as ties to these grants were essential in establishing true ownership of property. (Courtesy Harry Frank Guggenheim Foundation.)

5. Roads and Ferries to Daniel Island

Early settlers on Daniel Island were faced with an immediate challenge as they sought to travel to the city or move the goods and materials produced on the island to market. Like nearly everywhere else in the Lowcountry, the numerous wetlands and rivers presented obstacles to travel by traditional means. However, these same waterways offered their own opportunities for travel and had in fact been used for that purpose for thousands of years by the Native Americans. The rivers proved to be well suited for moving bulky and heavy materials from plantations to market.

The earliest Carolina shipbuilding focused on the local needs of moving goods along shallow rivers and creeks. Large, commercial shipyards would not become a mainstay of Charlestown industry until after the 1740s. Rather, early shipbuilding activity harnessed the local craftsmen's abilities and was generally a part of every large landowner's production. These early vessels were called canoe boats, or perigoes, and were made by joining two dugout cypress logs and fitting them with a keel, rudder, sails, and oars. They were capable of carrying 40 to 50 barrels of produce.

Privately built landings or piers provided points where these craft could dock. Two early landowners, Captain Daniell and Richard Codner, established piers on the Wando and Cooper Rivers, respectively. Early roads or paths on the island were built and maintained at the expense of the owners. By the turn of the 18th century, however, the Lords Proprietors of the province of Carolina recognized the need to formally lay out, build, and maintain public roads and bridges to unite the colony and allow for the rapid movement of information, commerce, and in times of alarm or crisis, troops. Funding for the roads came as a tax at "the equal charge and labor of all the male persons above the age of sixteen years and under sixty that lived or owned land on or adjacent to the road."

Acts ratified by the governing assembly in 1703, 1709, and 1712 created public roads on Daniel Island that supported owners on both the Wando and Cooper sides of the island. One road was to be created from Captain Daniell's plantation on Daniel Island to the Fogarty plantation at Cainhoy. Another was to connect the Codner plantation to the point where it joined the Daniell Road. A third was to provide access to Daniel Island from the plantation of George Smith, who lived on the Cooper River just south of Flagg Creek (called Cooke Creek in the late 1700s). The 1712 act also specifically mentions the bridge and causeway that was to be kept "in good and sufficient repair . . . over the Creek on the Northwest Side of the Island commonly called the Wading Place and to reimburse Robert Daniel Jr. who built and erected the bridge."

Ferries, vessels that charged a fee to carry people, livestock, and goods, began to appear nearly as soon as habitation spread out of Charlestown. Undoubtedly, ferry service ran from Daniel Island to the Charlestown neck early in the

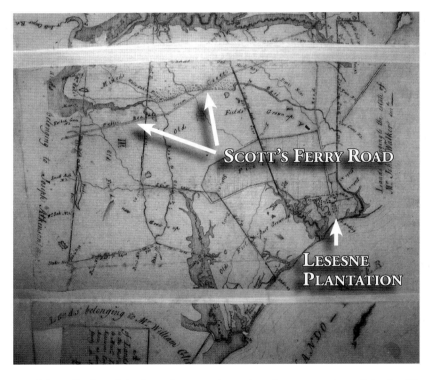

This 1784 Purcell plat of the Isaac Lesesne plantation shows a portion of the "public road from Scotts Ferry." This road was established in 1709 to join the Codner Ferry (now called Scotts Ferry) to Robert Daniell's settlement. This ferry and road became the primary route on the island and was in use throughout the Revolutionary War and into the 19th century. It crossed Little Beresford Creek near the sixth tee of the Beresford Creek Golf Course, a crossing that was used until 1995. The tape was added later along the document's original folds. (Courtesy Charleston County RMC.)

Pictured is a portion of Scotts Ferry Road today near the Cooper River.

18th century from the Codner plantation on the west side of the island. After Charlestown became a royal colony in 1720, the legislature began to determine where ferries could be operated from, the charges to be incurred for passages, penalties for failing to maintain a public ferry, and who was legally entitled to operate the ferry service. In 1731, the assembly granted Charles Codner, son of Richard Codner (one of the original landowners on Daniel Island), the right to operate a ferry from his estate to the lower bluff on the Neck, the present-day location of the old navy base. Two boats were to be kept for the ferry service, one on each side of the river. The round-trip fee for a man and a horse was 10 shillings, a single passenger five shillings, and each head of cattle 10 shillings.

By 1765, Joseph Scott had purchased the Codner plantation and was providing ferry service to Charlestown in addition to the same area on the Neck that Codner had been servicing. A term of service for 14 years had been granted. Fees to the Neck remained the same, while roundtrip fees to the docks at Charleston were 20 shillings per person and 20 shillings per horse.

In 1785, John Clement (1744–1801), who had been operating a ferry at Edisto Island, was granted permission to operate a ferry both to the Neck area and to the city piers for a term of 14 years. Clement was a Revolutionary War veteran, with both infantry and artillery units in the Charleston area. He is buried not far from the Daniell marker at St. Philip's in Charleston.

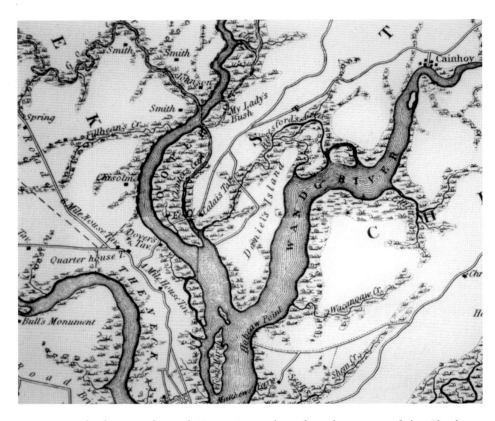

In 1820, Charles Vignoles and Henry Ravenel conducted a survey of the Charleston District that was included in the 1825 Mills Atlas. This map shows the location of Scotts Ferry Road, the public road and bridge across the marshes north of Daniel Island, and the new road to the ferry that John Clement was granted a charter to operate. Clement's ferry crossed both the Cooper River and Clouter Creek and included a causeway across the marsh between the Cooper and the creek.

The ferry's location was essentially the same as had been used by Codner and Scott, and was called Ityone Point. It is probable that Clement introduced a newer type of ferry boat. These vessels were basically flat, rectangular platforms of shallow draft and minimal freeboard, propelled by hand or tide and designed to operate in the relatively calm waters of Lowcountry rivers and sounds. Ferry landings that have been examined by archeologists have a shallow gradient that facilitates the use of a loading ramp to allow passengers, livestock, and wheeled vehicles such as carriages to board.

Clement significantly reduced the fees, which were now three shillings per person round trip to the city. Larger cargo, including carts, wagons, and livestock, seemed to be carried only to the landing on the west side of the Cooper River, referred to as Pleasant Bluff. An act specified that public roads were to be constructed leading to the landing at Pleasant Bluff and also granted Clement exclusive rights to operate ferries from the east side of the Cooper River.

Over the next seven years, Clement built at his own expense a causeway of considerable length that cut across the marsh and afforded a much more direct crossing from Clement's Ferry, as the western landing on the Neck was now called. In 1792, Clement was granted a seven year term to operate his ferry from the new location. He was also granted the right to operate a rope ferry across Clouter Creek. This type of ferry allowed easier passage, as an operator could pull himself across the creek and be kept from being moved upstream or downstream by the tidal currents. This new alignment of Clement's Ferry remained unchanged for the remainder of its life.

Clement also built taverns on each side of the Cooper River, one called Dover and the other Calais. Ferry owners and operators often built taverns and stables at their landings as ways to generate additional income from the passengers who often had to wait for the right combination of tide, wind, or current to make a passage possible or safe.

In 1815, John Spring and John Gordon, who owned a large brick-making operation on Thomas Island, purchased the ferry from the estate of John

In the early 1970s, Elias Bull conducted a survey of Charleston and Berkeley Counties for places and buildings of historical significance. This two-and-a-half-foot carved granite marker was cataloged by Bull and was one of a series that showed stagecoach drivers the distance to Calais Tavern, located on the eastern side of Clements Ferry. In 1793, John Clements obtained 15 acres on both sides of his ferry over the Cooper River and built a tavern, an inn, and a stable at both landings. The western landing was named Dover. This was a reference to the Dover-Calais ferry that crossed the English Channel at its narrowest point and reflected the large French Huguenot population east of the Cooper and the English population to the west. (Courtesy Charleston County Public Library, Charleston Room collections.)

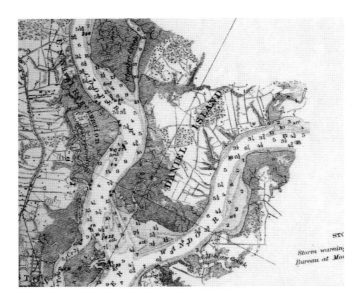

Coastal surveys conducted in the late 1800s did not cover areas as far inland as Daniel Island. This 1916 chart published by the U.S. Coast and Geodesic Survey, based on surveys conducted from 1849 to 1914, provides the first accurate view of the island before major transformations took place on the southern end later in the 20th century.

Clement Jr., who died in 1809, and were granted a 14-year permit to operate it. They also ensured that the road leading to their ferry was accessible from Daniel Island, and in 1821 an act was passed to revitalize and maintain the road across the marsh at the Wading Place. The ferry and its taverns were shown on a late 1863 map of Charleston, and both are believed to have continued operating until the end of the Civil War.

With the loss of Clement's Ferry, passage from the island now required traveling north to Strawberry Ferry to cross the Cooper River, or to Cainhoy to cross the Wando. The road across the marshes appears to have been maintained at least through the early 20th century, as the manager of the Cunningham cattle and agricultural operations on the island lived close to where the road left the island.

The advent of commercial truck farming on Daniel Island provided the impetus to again find easier and faster ways on and off the island. Shortly after the southern part of the island was purchased by the A. F. Young Company in 1905, three piers were built along the Wando River and one at Bellinger Island on Beresford's Creek. These piers were essential in getting perishable produce off the island to the railheads for shipment north, and were named after the farms they served: Scott Pier, Acme Pier, Mitchell Pier, and Pole Grove Pier (near the present-day sales center). The road across the marsh, always a challenge to keep in good working order, was allowed to fall into disrepair, and by the late 1940s it was barely visible in aerial photographs.

The island's roads still followed many of the paths that had existed since the early 1700s or the property lines that defined the 18th century plantations. There were no vehicles on the island and all work was done by horse, mule, or oxen. The sale of the operation to the American Fruit Growers did little to change the roads or access to the island. By the mid-1920s, a mail boat named the *Lucas* stopped at a pier near the present-day Childrens Park, and it provided passage to the city for a small fee. In 1940, the boat's name was *Euklid*, and its stop was moved to the Mitchell Pier complex where a small post office was built. The round-trip cost was 15¢. There was also a ferry operated by the American Fruit Growers called the *Blue Goose* and it too could be used by the managers who lived on the island for passage to the

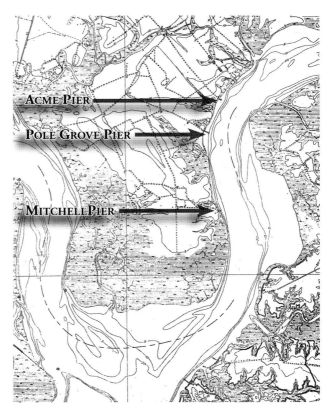

The U.S. War Department conducted extensive surveys of the coastal United States. This 1918 War Department chart shows the three piers that the A. F. Young company built or improved to support its truck-farming operations on Daniel Island. The piers were named for the farming areas they were associated with.

This dam and road structure in Cochran Park is evident in 1786 plats and was kept in good repair until the early 1990s. Dams such as this had multiple purposes throughout the history of the island. They were used to collect and hold freshwater from the few streams on Daniel Island, to provide a stable surface to cross marshy areas, and to keep tides from flooding land that could otherwise be used for crop production and ranching.

city. Vehicles on the island in 1940 included a Model T Ford, a White farm truck, and several tractors.

In the early part of the 20th century, those who worked on the island and lived on Thomas Island normally used a narrow wooden-plank causeway that ran a few feet above the marsh and ended at Beresford Creek just across from Bellinger Island. A small rowboat would then ferry four or five people at a time. In the late 1930s, the man who ran this boat was named Walter. Reverend Reilly believes that this was Isaac Walter Bellinger, who lived on Bellinger Island. For the workers who lived on Daniel Island, the ferries to the city were an option, but given the daily wage of 50¢ to $1 a day, the 15¢ price was prohibitive. Residents could also leave the island via the wooden footpath from Bellinger Island to Thomas Island.

Reverend Benjamin Dennis's father ran a steam ferry from the end of Thomas Island where Clements Ferry Road ends to the city docks, as well as to the fertilizer plant on the Cooper. This service ended, however, in 1939, when a bridge over the Wando at Cainhoy allowed car and truck traffic to reach Thomas Island. Shortly thereafter, a wooden bridge was built over

Beresford Creek, and residents had their first route off the island by road in 40 years. Reverend Dennis worked on the island from 1931 to 1938, and Philip Simmons, the highly accomplished blacksmith whose works grace numerous homes and garden gates in downtown Charleston and who was born on the island in 1912 and spent many summers helping his grandfather William "Wittey" Simmons work the farm in the 1930s, called this the "old way onto the Island." Simmons lived with his grandparents for the first eight years of his life on the Furman Track. Bob Tuten, who lived on the island from 1935 to 1941, remembers that a car that was kept in Charleston by the piers was moved to his house, and what a treat it was to drive from his home into the city to see *Gone with the Wind* with his family. The piers were still the primary way to move produce off the island, although by 1940 the pier at Pole Grove had been abandoned.

In 1946, after Harry F. Guggenheim purchased the southern 3,000 acres of Daniel Island, massive changes were made to the roads and to the topography of the island. Exiting roads were straightened, and many were removed. This road structure remained intact on the island even after the opening of the Mark Clark Expressway in 1992. It was not until 1994 that the present-day roads began to be constructed.

In 1939, bridges were installed over Beresford and Little Beresford Creeks. They provided the first vehicular access to the island since the end of the Civil War. A road was also established through a wooded and marshy area to connect the bridges to the central north-south road on the island near the blacksmith's shed and a deep well. This was Cainhoy Road, which terminated at the Mitchell Pier complex on the Wando River. (Courtesy USDA.)

65

In 1780, the British captured the city of Charlestown and began to fortify strategic approaches to the city by building small redoubts and stationing troops where they could be readily deployed against the Colonial militia. This brick and cement structure measures four feet by five feet by four feet deep and had a cement floor. It is located on the Cooper River approach to Scotts Ferry on high land and is surrounded by defensive trenches. Structures such as these were used to provide secure storage for gunpowder, small-arms ammunition, and small field-piece shells.

6. DANIEL ISLAND'S FREEDOM FIGHTERS

While Daniel Island has not been the site of any battles in any of the conflicts that took place on U.S. soil, its location at the confluence of the Cooper and Wando Rivers has made it strategically important to the defenses of the City of Charleston over the centuries. Additionally, many who have served in the nation's wars have lived on and in some instances are buried on the island.

The Revolutionary War

During the early years of the Carolina colony's existence, the roads and ferries of Daniel Island allowed rapid communication of approaching danger to the colony's leaders, and provided a way to move militia into the interior portions of the colony. Governor Daniell was elected to lead repeated expeditions in defense of the colony against both the Spanish and several Native American uprisings.

Just 70 years later, the turmoil of the Revolutionary War swirled around and across Daniel Island. In early 1780, the British landed at Seabrook Island and began a slow and methodical advance on Charlestown, a city that they had failed to capture by sea in 1776. Colonial leaders tried to fortify many of the approaches to the city, and quickly recognized the strategic importance of the Scotts Ferry road.

General Lincoln, the American officer in charge of the continental forces in South Carolina, planned to strengthen the Cooper River approaches to Scotts Public Road at Scotts Ferry. His objective was to ensure that the supply routes to Charlestown from the farms and plantations on Daniel Island and from the upper reaches of St. Thomas and St. Denis Parish remained open even as the British pressed towards the city from the east. He was also responding to the pleas of the residents who had businesses and homes on the island and were sympathetic to the American cause.

However, before he could complete his plans, British Lt. Col. Banestre Tarleton was ordered by Lieutenant General Cornwallis to engage the

SOUTH-CAROLINA

PURSUANT to an ACT of the GENERAL ASSEMBLY passed the 16th of March, 1783, We, the COMMISSIONERS of the TREASURY, have this day delivered to

Mr Joseph Atkinson

this our INDENTED CERTIFICATE for the Sum of *Nineteen Hundred & Nineteen pounds Seven shillings & sixpence Sterling, for hire of the Brigantine Bellona & disbursements in 1779; For the Brigantine Wasp and Disbursements in 1779; For Provisions & 47 days hire of the Brigand in ——— 1779; ———————*

the said *Joseph Atkinson*

his Executors, Administrators, or Assigns will be entitled to receive from this Office the Sum of *One Hundred and Thirty four pounds Seven Shillings and one Penny Sterling* — for one Year's Interest on the Principal Sum of *Nineteen hundred & Nineteen Pounds Seven Shillings and Sixpence Sterling* and the like Interest Annually *by Resolution of the Gen.l Assembly 1783*

The said *Joseph Atkinson* his Executors, Administrators or Assigns, will be entitled also to receive, and shall be paid, if demanded, the principal Sum of *Nineteen hundred & Nineteen hundred Seven Shillings & Sixpence Sterling* on the *Sixth day of July 1786.* And the said *Joseph Atkinson* his Executors, Administrators, or Assigns, may make any Purchases at any Public Sales of Confiscated Property, (except such as shall be ordered by the Legislature for special Purposes;) and this INDENT shall be received in Payment.

For the true performance of the several payments in manner abovementioned, the PUBLIC TREASURY is made liable, and the FAITH of the STATE pledged by the aforesaid ACT.

GIVEN under our Hands at the TREASURY-OFFICE, in CHARLESTON, the *Sixth* Day of *July* — one thousand seven hundred and eighty *four*

Commissioners

The states generally reimbursed citizens for provisions, materials, and other services that were used by continental forces during the Revolutionary War. These receipts, or warrants, were audited and consolidated into a single debt statement. Joseph Atkinson, who owned land to the west of Governor Daniell's settlement during the war, was issued this certificate in July 1784 for, among other items, lumber provided to Colonel Creighton in March 1780 and the use of the brigantine Bellona, brigantine Wasp in 1779, and the sloop Tammy in 1780. Payment was totaled at £1,919 and 7 shillings, with an interest of £134 and 7 shillings to be paid annually starting in 1783, payable in full in July 1786. (Courtesy South Carolina Archives.)

American forces, primarily its cavalry, along the Cooper River. On April 14, 1780, Tarleton attacked at night and annihilated the American cavalry and foot soldiers under the command of Col. William Washington and Gen. Isaac Huger at Biggin's Bridge, a primary crossing point on the west branch of the Cooper River about 10 miles north of Daniel Island. Thirty Americans were killed and another 60 were captured. They also lost forty wagons of ammunition, horse equipage, food, and clothing, as well as 98 horses. These horses became mounts for the British calvary in South Carolina, which was in desperate need of good horses.

All roads leading west and south from Charlestown were already under British control, and the destruction of the only viable fighting force at Biggin's Bridge effectively gave the British control of the lands to the north and east as well. It also enabled them to focus on tightening their control of the city, particularly the roads and ferries that supplied Charlestown from Daniel Island and Mount Pleasant, without real fear of a counterattack.

Cornwallis knew that the protracted siege of the city would continue as long as provisions continued to flow into it. He was also aware of a sizable force of colonial troops and militia that had left Virginia and was making its way south to help defend Charlestown. It was particularly bothersome for him to learn that even though General Lincoln had on April 22 ordered the meat ration within the besieged city reduced from one pound a day to three-fourths of a pound, on April 24, enough fresh meat was obtained from Daniels Island that the full ration was restored.

On April 25, Cornwallis ordered Tarleton to take Daniel Island and ensure that he destroyed any stores that would be of use to the colonial forces. This order, however, was somewhat problematic for Cornwallis. Tarleton, whose portrayal in the movie *The Patriot* as a cruel and merciless commander was historically accurate, had a reputation for brutal warfare that was well known within the British command. Cornwallis knew that American passions would be inflamed by atrocities committed against civilians, so in his order to Tarleton he pointedly remarked that he "must recommend it to you in the strongest manner to use your utmost endeavors to prevent the troops under your command from committing irregularities."

Tarleton raided Daniel Island on April 28, 1780, driving off all the cattle and destroying a great deal of provisions that "scarcely left anything for those remaining on the plantations." He also left a small garrison to ensure that no passage from Scotts Ferry could take place. Similar action along the Cooper

River on the Mount Pleasant side effectively isolated Charlestown from all outside support. On May 9, a truce was declared so that terms could be arranged for the surrender of the city. On May 12, 1780, the city surrendered, due in no small part to its inability to provide food for it occupants.

Cornwallis continued to solidify his control over South Carolina and directed Tarleton to the northern part of the state to meet the American reinforcements who were known to be near the North Carolina border. On May 29, Tarleton met the American forces at the Battle of Waxhaws. The British resoundingly defeated this force, and historians portray their slaughter of American troops as they tried to surrender as a key turning point that unified much of the uncommitted colonial population in rebellion against British rule. It was from this battle that Col. Francis Marion began to effectively recruit local militia, which engaged in guerilla warfare against the British from the nearly impenetrable swamps and marshes of the Lowcountry and whose actions earned him the name "Swamp Fox."

Marion's raids included several onto British-occupied Daniel Island. Under the command of Col. Wade Hampton, a calvary raid occurred in July 1781 that may have included Isaac Lesesne Jr., who had joined the regiment of state calvary and fought under the command of Francis Marion on several occasions. On Friday, August 24, 1781, a body of militia under the command of Capt. William Bennett and supported by continental horse, made an incursion into St. Thomas parish. A contingent came down to Daniel Island and plundered the plantation of the Loyalist widow Mrs. Elfe and continued to Lesesne's plantation, where they destroyed all of the effects of the Loyalist Mr. Balfour that they could find.

The British considered the ferry and roads of Daniel Island essential to their continued ability to retain control of the city. They reinforced the landing along the Cooper River and stationed galleys, or small sailing ships armed with cannon, near the Scott Ferry Landing and in the Wando. The Wando location was most likely near the Lesesne or Daniel estates, as both locations had docks that would allow the ships to be provisioned. These ships were not Royal Navy vessels, but privateers. Local Loyalist businessmen had obtained the vessels and sold their services to the British as commerce raiders and to protect vital British interests.

This ability to secure Daniel Island enabled the British to forage for food and wood, as well as to launch attacks against American militia and regular forces that were gaining control of the nearby countryside.

On Jan 2, 1782, Maj. William Brereton crossed the Cooper River and landed at Scotts Ferry with 350 infantry and calvary with orders from the British commandant of Charleston, Maj. Gen. Alexander Leslie, to engage Francis Marion's detachments, which were gathering north of the city. Brereton continued across the island and proceeded up the public road and across Beresford Creek before camping on the Cainhoy Peninsula that night. The next morning, the British forces engaged an American force led by Col. Richard Richardson Jr., resulting in the defeat of the colonial forces.

Shortly after this battle, the British established a permanent garrison on Daniel Island along the Wando River at the Lesesne Plantation site. On February 24, 1782, Colonel Thompson, the local commander, led forces composed of cavalry, militia, and one three-pounder field piece off of Daniel Island in an attack on the American troops stationed at Wambaw Bridge. The ensuing battle was another defeat for the American forces, who fled into the countryside after putting up stiff resistance.

Following the Revolutionary War, the individual states began paying the debts incurred by citizens as they supported the continental army and the local militia. Warrants had been issued throughout the conflict and signed by local commanders in the field as they procured grain, livestock, foodstuffs, cotton, wood, and the services of those who owned boats and sailing craft. These warrants were audited and a letter of credit was drafted that enabled payment to be made over a period of time. The South Carolina warrants are held in the state archives in Columbia and include nearly all the Daniel Island landholders who supported American independence. These include Thomas and Robert Cochran, Barnard Beekman, Isaac Lesesne, Sarah Daniell, Edmond Bellinger, William and John Glen, Joseph Addison, and William Scott.

Daniel Island's Ghost

In 1935, the federal government commissioned a Federal Writers Project as part of the New Deal under the auspices of the Works Progress Administration. The Federal Writers Project employed over 20,000 writers during its tenure, providing 48 state guides and many other special works. One of these was *The Ocean Highway*, which chronicled the history, resources, and points of interest along the highway that stretched from New Brunswick, New Jersey to Jacksonville, Florida. When they arrived in Charleston in 1936, the writers noted three points of significance: the Cooper River Bridge, which had opened in 1929, and Hog and Daniel Islands, which were both viewable from the crest of the bridge. They also mentioned that the residents of "Daniell's Island" described "a local ghost—a British Soldier in full uniform of Revolutionary times, who rides about on Horseback."

Philip Simmons remembers his grandfather Wittey Simmons and other "old ones" talking about just such a ghost. Simmons said that according to them, it was usually seen at dusk or just as the sun was rising. He also remembers that his grandfather was severely reprimanded as a child for believing in ghosts. He had to write on the board at Sunday school many times, "only Jesus rose from the dead."

Civil War and the U.S. Colored Infantry

Daniel Island did not see any direct military action during the Civil War. The lines of defense created by the Confederate forces relied upon earthworks across the Charleston Neck and the Cooper River to act as a barrier to Northern troops. A line of "torpedoes," or barrels filled with explosives, was strung across the Wando River between Daniel Island and the lands near Hobcaw. No ships or troops were stationed on the island.

However, the men and women of Daniel Island were involved in the war. Early on, there was a strong desire in some parts of the Union army to allow African Americans to become soldiers and fight in the war. Some officers tried to form regiments of black volunteers, but the War Department forced these units to disband. In July 1862, the U.S. Congress passed a law allowing blacks to serve as laborers, cooks, or wagon drivers. The law still did not allow black soldiers. In August 1862, the War Department decided to officially allow the army to recruit blacks. It also said that any slave who fought would be declared free. This meant freedom for their wives and children, too.

All states were allowed to recruit and form regiments of black soldiers, and the popular film *Glory* chronicled the formation of one such regiment, the 54th Massachusetts. The first two regiments formed in South Carolina were the 1st South Carolina and the 2nd South Carolina Volunteer Infantry, which were later designated United States Colored Infantry. On March 10, 1863, these two regiments occupied Jacksonville, Florida with no resistance. They repulsed several attacks by Confederate forces, but their isolated location far from Union supply lines and support eventually led the Federal forces to abandon the city.

The War Department continued to support the recruitment and training of all African Americans, and instituted a new numbering system. Eventually, the Union established approximately 160 regiments and 10 batteries of light artillery comprised of over 200,000 ex-slaves and freemen, or about 10 percent of the U.S. Army during the Civil War. The 1st South Carolina and 2nd South Carolina were combined with a regiment of white soldiers and redesignated the 33rd United States Colored Troops on February 8, 1864. South Carolina eventually formed six regiments, the 21st, 33rd, 34th, 103rd, 104th, and 128th, and one artillery battery, Battery G, 2nd Light Artillery Regiment, with more than 5,000 African Americans recruited.

Daniel Island has ties to two of these regiments. Private David Sparkman was a member of the 33rd regiment, U.S. Colored Troops, and was the great-great-grandfather of Reverend David Reilly, who today is helping to maintain the three African American cemeteries on the island. Reilly's relatives also include the Bellingers, who are buried on the island. The 33rd assaulted and captured Battery Gregg on James Island on July 2, 1864. In December of that year they coordinated with the 55th Massachusetts at the battle of Honey Hill, which ended as a costly defeat for the Federal forces. In their final year, they were part of a garrison that guarded both Charleston and Savannah, Georgia.

According to this grave marker, G. C. Coxswain was a member of Company K, 103rd colored infantry regiment. Little else is known about this African American soldier who served with the Union army during the Civil War.

William Brailsford is interred in the Lesesne cemetery. He was a third lieutenant, Beat Company Number 2, in the 16th Regiment of the South Carolina Militia, Charleston District. Prior to the war he was a surveyor, working primarily in the Colleton and Beaufort districts.

Private Sparkman was assigned to garrison duty in Charleston, and the legacy of the end of the war has been preserved within the Reilly family. When word of the end of the war reached Charleston, Sparkman was part of a squad that began to spread the word and search for any Confederate soldiers still in hiding. Dressed in the distinctive red pants of the 33rd, his squad attracted a throng of cheering citizens. According to Reilly family tradition, each step they took resounded with a single word, "freedom." Freedom for Charlestonians, who were now able to accept the end of a war that had destroyed their city, and more importantly, freedom for all African Americans. As word reached Daniel Island, families banged pots, pans, and scrub boards and sang. Women were waving long dresses in joy and celebration. Daniel Sparkman was mustered out of the service on February 9, 1866, and lived on Daniel Island until his death.

The second local tie is to the 103rd U.S. Colored Troops. G. C. Coxswain, who achieved the rank of corporal, is buried in the Simmons Cemetery. The 103rd was organized at Hilton Head, South Carolina on March 10, 1865, and attached to the District of Savannah, Department of the South. It performed garrison and guard duties at Savannah and at various points in Georgia and South Carolina. They were mustered out of the army in April 1866.

There is one final tie from the Civil War to Daniel Island. Peter F. Stevens, who was born in Florida in 1830, entered the Citadel in Charleston in 1846 and after several postings became the superintendent of the Citadel in 1859. In 1861, Governor Pickens ordered Stevens and a detachment of cadets to man a battery on Morris Island and to fire on any vessel bearing an American flag entering the harbor. The result was the firing upon the *Star of the West*, the first act of aggression in the coming conflict. In August 1861, Stevens resigned from his position at the Citadel and organized the Holcombe Legion. He was wounded at Sharpsburg and resigned from the service in October 1862. He later became the bishop of the Reformed Episcopal Church in Charleston.

As bishop, Stevens oversaw a diverse number of churches including St. Luke's Reformed Episcopal Church on Daniel Island. This church was located on the present-day sixth fairway on the Beresford Creek golf course. Reverend Dennis, Reverend Reilly, and Philip Simmons all remember attending that church, and their parents and grandparents talked often about Bishop Stevens coming to the island to confirm new members into the faith.

Pictured is Cunningham's steamer at Scott Pier. This 50-ton coal-fired ship was kept operational for several years after Cunningham's death and was finally sold in 1905 for $435. (Courtesy the Daniel Island Company.)

7. Consolidation and Truck Farming

The Civil War devastated the economy of the South. Charleston was a city in ruins. In addition to the devastation of the war, a severe earthquake in 1865 had destroyed much of the city's buildings. With the abolishment of slavery much of the economic base, which had depended upon slave labor, was severely shaken. Most of Daniel Island fell into non-productive use and many of the holdings were sold or confiscated for non-payment of debt. Wealthy families were able to buy land and consolidate small holdings into sizable tracts that could be farmed or used to raise livestock. On Daniel Island, consolidation occurred fairly rapidly, and by 1880 there were only two landholders. The Furman family owned just over 1,000 acres on the northern part of the island, while the southern lands were owned by George Cunningham.

George Cunningham

A native of Tennessee, Cunningham arrived in the Charleston area in 1852 and within a year had become involved in the cattle and butchery business. A successful businessman, he also got involved in local politics during the difficult years of Reconstruction and served in a number of local and federal positions, including alderman in 1868. Cunningham was twice elected mayor for terms of two years each from 1873 to 1877. A staunch Republican, he presided over the city during extremely turbulent times that included a riot in nearby Cainhoy in October 1876 between armed black Republicans and white Democrats during a political meeting there. Another riot occurred in the city a month later that was also politically motivated and again pitted whites against blacks. Cunningham was chairman of the Board of the County Commissioners of Charleston County from 1872 to 1878, and was appointed a U.S. marshall in 1889.

Cunningham also actively acquired land in the Charleston area, particularly on Daniel Island. By April 1876, he had purchased 2,938 acres, or approximately 65 percent of the 4,144 total acres on the island. This large tract comprised the southern two thirds of Daniel Island and would remain intact under several owners for the next 115 years, until development of the island commenced in 1995.

Phillip Simmons and Reverend David Reilly have strong ties to Daniel Island. Simmons was born on the island on June 9, 1912 and lived there with his grandfather until he moved to Charleston in 1920. His cousin Reverend Reilly has relatives buried on the island in the Simmons cemetery and has worked for the past three decades to clean up and preserve the four cemeteries on Daniel Island. The two are pictured in Simmons's office.

Cunningham raised livestock to support his butchery business in downtown Charleston. In 1886, he had 13 horses, 30 head of cattle, and 10 sheep and goats. However, the primary focus of his holdings on Daniel Island was the production of sea island cotton. Many thousands of bales were shipped from the island to the main docks at Charleston during his tenure, from landings and piers along both the Wando River and Beresford Creek.

The property was divided into smaller farms or units that had a manager who oversaw the operations of a resident labor force that had grown from just a few families to nearly a dozen by 1902. These African American families paid mortgages for their homes, and provided a year-round workforce that tended to the livestock and fields. A migrant workforce was hired to help plant the cotton and harvest it, a practice that was common in the Lowcountry at the turn of the 20th century and that would continue in Daniel Island agriculture until after World War II.

George Cunningham died intestate in 1902, and probate court records show that there were nine families who lived on his land and were paying mortgages.

These families were headed by John Pickens, James Dennis, Benjamin Bellinger, John Campbell, William Kinlock, Richard Pickens, Nathanial Kinlock, Isaac Bellinger, and Frank Campbell. Wittey Simmons, Lawrence McCoy, and Sam Brown are also listed as having earned wages for planting, harvesting, packing, and shipping cotton, and for tending to the livestock on the island.

Truck Farming

In 1905, George Cunningham's heirs sold his land to A. F. Young and Company for $15,000. The New York company established the largest truck-farming operation in the Lowcountry on Daniel Island in the early 1900s. The name "truck" can be misleading when discussing these vegetable farms. It comes from the middle English word "trukken," which referred to a barter or trading system that did not involve cash. In the Lowcountry after the Civil War, cash

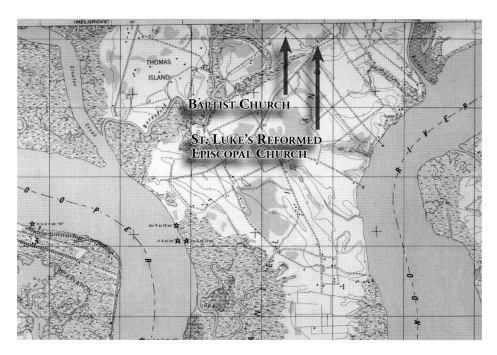

In 1943, the U.S. Army published this chart of Charleston that was based on 1941 aerial photography and surveys conducted in 1918. It was classified "restricted" shortly after the bombing of Pearl Harbor and was not released for general use until a decade later. It shows the location of the Baptist and Reformed Episcopal Churches on Daniel Island.

Mules were the primary means of plowing fields and pulling carts around Daniel Island for the majority of the truck-farming era. Collars were in constant need of repair, and a skilled craftsman was needed to make sure it was done right. This photo was taken in the early 1930s in southern Berkeley County. (Courtesy Library of Congress.)

was in short supply, so many farmers raised vegetables on small farms and traded them with neighbors or in town for the other goods they needed.

A. F. Young created a subsidiary for its Charleston operations called the Daniel Island Truck Farms. Several years were spent preparing the fields for intensive vegetable growing, and the first crop was grown in 1908. By 1910, conversion to a large-scale commercial truck farm operation was complete. Three piers were built on the Wando River to allow rapid transportation to market in Charleston. The Acme Pier was to the east of the present-day Family Circle Cup complex, Pole Grove Pier was at the present-day location of the pier by the sales center, and Mitchell Pier was to the east of present-day Smythe Park. A warehouse complex was also built at Mitchell that was composed of two large buildings where potatoes were sorted and packed by grade, and other products were also prepared for shipment. This pier extended into the Wando River, but was not long enough to reach deep water at low tide. Bricks were scavenged from other locations on the island, and a solid walkway was built along the pier extending into the marsh for at least 10 yards. A set of railroad tracks ran along the pier and through the first packing house, into a second packing house directly behind it. Produce gathered during the day was sorted for size and quality and stored until the daily barge arrived to pick it up.

The company also built a significant number of small homes to support the resident labor force. These are shown on a 1918 War Department map of Daniel Island. Two of these houses survived until 1995, including one that was still occupied in 1994. These were company-owned buildings and the families who lived in them did not pay rent or have their wages garnished. However, all adults were expected to work only on Daniel Island and to be available "as needed, for as long as needed" to support the operations of the farms. The homes were comprised of four rooms including two bedrooms, a kitchen, and a living room that could also be used as a bedroom. Each home had a brick fireplace for heating in the winter months. Several homes were also built for the managers of the individual farm units. These had larger rooms for living and sleeping, as well as an additional room for dining. None of them had running water, electricity, or indoor plumbing.

The company managed the land in eight small units, keeping the same names Cunningham used: Center, Scott, 15 Acre, Barfield, Isaac, Mitchell, Pole Grove, and Acme. Asparagus, cabbage, cucumbers, potatoes, and beans were the primary crops grown for sale in northern states. After these were harvested, corn and sweet potatoes were planted for use as livestock feed. In 1917, the Daniel Island subsidiary was folded back into A. F. Young, in part because of a crop failure the previous year caused by a fertilizer shortage. By 1920, 1,000 acres were drained and under cultivation, supporting truck crops of cabbages, cucumbers, and Irish (or white) potatoes.

Truck farms frequently changed ownership, and in 1921 American Fruit Growers, a company based in Pittsburgh and Los Angeles, purchased the

The Blue Goose label was the trademark of the American Fruit Growers Company and it was on every box of cabbage and every bag of potatoes that left the island.

Hundreds of workers were employed during the harvest of cabbage and white potatoes. Workers were paid per barrel or bag of potatoes and crate of cabbage picked. Tokens such as this were given to the workers in the field. At the end of the week workers would turn these in and be given cash for their labor. One 55-gallon barrel earned 20¢. (Courtesy the Daniel Island Company.)

Daniel Island property from A. F. Young. American Fruit Growers invested heavily in the Daniel Island operation. A packing shed was constructed on Beresford Creek on Bellinger Island, and additional infrastructure was built at Mitchell Pier including a general store, a post office, a school, and additional houses for the manager of the store and the captain of the American Fruit Growers passenger boat, the *Blue Goose.*

The company also brought in a full-time overseer in 1922 who was skilled in soil science and fertilizers to help optimize the yields of the farms. Harry Hetzel of the Hagerstown, Maryland production division of American Fruit Growers became the permanent overseer of the farms' operations. Hetzel raised the productivity of the island's land to twice that of other South Carolina farms where white potatoes and cabbage were grown. By 1937, 63 railcars of cabbage were produced from 150 acres, and 37,000 barrels of white potatoes where produced from 500 acres. In 1945, an additional 200 acres of cabbage were added, which was a very profitable crop for the company. These gains in production lands were made possible by the introduction of gasoline-powered tractors, which allowed fields to be planted much more efficiently than with mules and oxen. American Fruit Growers maintained truck farming operations on Daniel Island until 1945, when the property was purchased by John Maybank for $65,000.

Throughout much of the truck farming era, no vehicular access to Daniel Island was possible until the Wando River bridge opened in July 1939 and the Cainhoy Road bridges over Beresford Creek opened in 1940. Horses, mules, and oxen were the primary tools for plowing the fields or moving large amounts of material around the island. Philip Simmons remarked that his grandfather's primary animals were oxen. He remembers Irish potatoes being the main crop he helped harvest as a young boy, and the very large peanuts that grew on Rodents Island.

The roads were all unpaved and followed the historical property lines established in the 1700s. Today, many of those same property lines are evident in the treelines and stands of live oak that were preserved during the development of the island.

Reverend Benjamin Dennis

Reverend Dennis lives just off Daniel Island on Clements Ferry Road on part of a 22-acre tract that his father acquired in the early 1920s for 50¢ an acre. He grew up "off island" but worked here as an adolescent for 18 months beginning in 1937. His parents and paternal grandparents lived and worked on Daniel Island, and his father and grandparents are buried on the island. He shared the following recollections about his time on Daniel Island during the truck-farming era.

"Daniel Island was the salvation of poor people, black and white," said Reverend Dennis. During the harvest season, the number of workers on the island expanded considerably. The need for additional labor to harvest the crops was provided by people who lived as far away as Huger and McClellanville. Most slept in tents during the harvest season. Work here provided a good source of money in an area where work, especially in the years following the Depression and even until the end of World War II, was very challenging to find.

Left: *The remains of the Mitchell Pier today.* Right: *The remains of the Acme Pier today.*

Four of the early 1900s tenant/manager dwellings remained on Daniel Island until they were torn down in the 1990s. This tenant house was near present-day Center Park on Daniel Island Drive (The Cain Hoy Road) and in 1972 was called the "Alston house." (Courtesy Brockington and Associates.)

By 1935, two principal crops were grown on Daniel Island. Cabbage was ready for cutting in June. In July and early August potatoes where harvested by a team of two workers. One drove the mule that pulled a plow that turned the soil and uncovered the potatoes. The other put the potatoes into a barrel or bag. No potatoes were unearthed in the middle of the day from 11:00 to 1:00, as they did not want the potatoes being harmed or burned by the sun.

The daily wage of the head of a household who lived on Daniel Island year-round was generally 40¢ to 50¢ per day. Additional money could be earned by family members, who would be paid by the bag or box of produce picked. A barrel of potatoes would earn about 10¢.

There was a large packing and sorting building on Bellinger Island. Several men operated the machine that sorted the potatoes into grades before they were packed into bags for shipping to Charleston. Reverend Dennis remembers a barge and tug called the *Dottle* that stopped daily near high tide to be loaded.

Dennis worked on Scott Farm for Bob Tuten, who later was replaced by his brother Eddie Tuten. Few workers lived on the island and most had to cross Beresford Creek to get to work, using the narrow plank bridge and small skiff to come across from Thomas Island. Workers would yell for Walter and he would row over to the walkway and then row them over to Daniel Island.

Although he did not live on the island, Dennis frequently visited friends who lived on the Furman Track, which even at that time still contained a significant number of African American homes. Yards then did not have grass, and the areas around the home were kept clear of weeds by constant hoeing. Food was plentiful in the summer, and families usually took turns cooking for the children. Each family was allowed to plant vegetables on land near their homes for their personal use. Rice was grown as well, and the husks were removed by placing the rice in a wooden vessel and pounding the rice with a rounded wooden timber.

Also located at the Mitchell Pier complex was a large general store that was referred to as "the big store." Here one could buy all the necessary working harnesses, and the boots, overalls, and jackets that would be needed by the workforce. Food was also available, but generally this supplemented what was grown on the land not under company cultivation. The store also sold bicycles, and Dennis remembers that they carried two brands: a Topps, which was smaller, and a Clawson, which was bigger. The store would withhold 50¢ a week from a worker's pay to be used for credit. In a year's time, Dennis had earned enough to get one of the Clawson bikes. Kerosene, used for lighting, was 2¢ per quart.

Dennis worked in fields where the Cochran Park and Etiwan Park neighborhoods have been built. He primarily harvested white potatoes and

This structure was located at the Mitchell Pier complex and was used to store mule collars and horse bridles and saddles during the truck-farming era. It was damaged during Hurricane Hugo, but still served as an equipment storage area until it was torn down in late 1998. (Courtesy Brockington and Associates.)

The Bridge House on Brady Island was home to the manager of the Bridge Farm during the American Fruit Growers era. Under Guggenheim, the manager of the cattle ranch lived here, including the Robert Murray family from 1960 to 1969. This house was severely damaged by Hurricane Hugo and torn down in 1995, when the Daniel Island Investment Company built new roads across Brady Island to support the increased traffic that development would bring. (Courtesy Brockington and Associates.)

either drove the mule or gathered the uncovered potatoes and put them in the barrels. One could ride the mule from the manager's house, where they were kept at night, to the field, but riding back after a day's work was forbidden.

Violence and fear were still a part of life on Daniel Island in the late 1930s. Black families who lived on the island rent-free were expected to remain on the island for employment. For a while a man named Saul would leave the island before sunrise and return after dark in order to work at the Etiwan Fertilizer Plant, where he could make significantly more money than by working on the island. One night Earl Stanley, a manager of the Mitchell Farm, shot Saul in the leg as he was returning. Dennis's time on the island ended in 1938 when he improperly attached a collar to the mule that was plowing potatoes, which ended up killing the mule. A farm manager by the name of Rudolph saw the mule go down and charged after Dennis on his horse. Reverend Dennis, 13 years old at the time, feared for his life and ran to Beresford Creek and swam across it.

Schools were provided for the workers' families. Segregation meant that there was a white school and a black school. The white school was a one-room building in the Mitchell Pier area, southwest of Smythe Park Lake. In 1935, seven children attended, with Berkeley County providing a teacher who came on Monday and left on Friday morning. In 1939, only two children attended, and in 1940, after the opening of the bridge over Beresford Creek, children attended school in Monks Corner.

The black school was in St. Luke's Reformed Episcopal Church, which was across the marsh from the present-day sixth tee on Beresford Creek Golf Course. School was four-and-a-half days long, with Friday being a half day so the teacher could return home for the weekend. Classes were only held for three months in the winter, when the working demands on the island were minimal. After the roads were completed in 1939, the Shingler School was opened near the present-day Cainhoy Fire Station on Clements Ferry Road. This building did not have glass windows, and boards were used to cover the openings in the cold months. Often, three to five boys would be sent out to gather firewood to heat the building before lessons could start.

The opening of the road also meant that demand for ferry service from the end of Clements Ferry Road ended. Reverend Dennis's father owned two boats that provided ferry service both to downtown Charleston and to the Etiwan Fertilizer plant.

Several homes were built in the early 1920s and modernized over time to include electricity and running water. This house was located at the Mitchell Pier complex and housed the Blue Goose captain and mechanic during the American Fruit Growers era. It was occupied into the early 1990s by various managers and caretakers of later cattle and truck farming operations, and was removed in 1999. (Courtesy Brockington and Associates.)

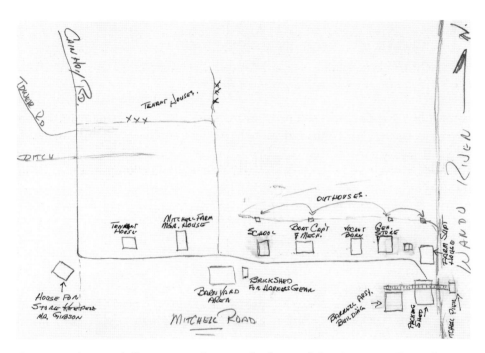

In 1939, the Mitchell Pier complex was the heart of the American Fruit Growers operations. By 1937, bags were used to ship potatoes and barrels were no longer needed. A warehouse full of barrel staves was used as firewood by the supervisor of the island. Produce was picked up both by a ship named Thelma and a tug named Doe Doe that pushed a barge. Tide constrained pickup times as the pier did not extend into deep water. (Courtesy Bob Tuten.)

8. A Year on Daniel Island c. 1938

Bob Tuten moved to Daniel Island with his family in 1935. His father Robert operated Bard Farm, one of six truck farms on the island at the time. Through multiple interviews, Tuten generously offered this rare glimpse into daily life on Daniel Island during its truck-farming days.

We will begin with the "hog killing time" of the year. This is when all the crops have been gathered, the potatoes banked, and all necessary chores completed for the oncoming winter. Hog killing time is usually late December or early January. The time of year when it is cold, usually below freezing temperatures. And it did get cold on Daniel Island.

Some of the manager's houses had cast iron wood-burning space heaters. They may have been part of the house or possibly purchased by the individual. Those heaters could be stoked with wood at night for some warmth next morning. A fireplace had to burn down before we went to bed as a precaution against sparks. The floors were of pine wood. The first thing mom or dad would do on a cold morning was to start a fire in the fireplace before building a fire in the cook stove. We kept plenty of kindling on hand for a quick start. The wood was sawed in early fall. Two workers and a crosscut saw would cut a pine one-and-a-half to two-and-a-half feet in diameter. Then they cut logs in lengths for the fireplace and the cook stove. These logs were piled in the yard and split by the barnyard man, stacked for drying, etc. Cooking heat was controlled by the amount of wood and a damper that controlled air supply.

A person was assigned to each of the managers who took care of the barnyard and animals and also took care of some of our household tasks like keeping the house supplied with wood and bringing water, from the well in our case, to the kitchen and back porch where soap and towels were kept for wash-up prior to coming into the house. We had a well near the south end of the house. It was not lined with brick. I remember bluish-grey clay walls. Some of the other houses had a pump nearby or on a porch. This water was for all purposes other than drinking. Our drinking water was hauled in kegs or glass jugs from the well near the blacksmith. The local water was drinkable but had a brackish taste.

Near the well on the south end of our house was a large (15 to 20 gallon) cast iron wash pot. This is where our laundry was done. The water was heated by a wood fire to a boiling temperature. The clothes were boiled and stirred for a period of time then removed to a galvanized #2 washtub which had rinse water. Sometimes the

SMYTHE PARK LAKE ISLAND

In this photograph of the Mitchell Pier complex in 1949, many of the American Fruit Growers buildings had been removed, including the big store, the school, and several managers' homes. The pier is in good repair, and the large packing shed and barrel-assembly barn are present, although not in use. A tram line ran through them to allow more rapid loading of the produce onto the barge for transport to the South Street Pier in Charleston. (Courtesy U.S. Department of Agriculture.)

clothes requiring additional scrubbing were put in another tub with hot water and soap and scrubbed on what was known as a washboard. After rinsing, the clothes were hung on a wire line to dry. In the wintertime they often froze on the line.

Each farm manager had his pick of two hogs, possibly more, the pick being made earlier in the year. Naturally this pick got the best of attention in food. A few months before killing time the selected hogs were kept penned and fed abundantly to fatten, as we called it. These animals must have been a money crop as well as cabbage and potatoes. I remember a barge at the pier on Bellinger's Island with a fence of wooden planks around the edge. The hogs were loaded here for transport to Charleston.

When butchering day came, a 55-gallon steel drum was buried in the ground at a 45-degree angle so as to hold a lot of water. Water was heated to a scalding temperature in the iron clothes wash pot and poured into the drum. But prior to this I was allowed to be the executioner. My father showed me the spot between the eyes and handed me the 22 rifle. It was a very easy job because the hog would stand there and look you in the eye.

The next task was to get the dead hog from the pen in the barnyard to the scalding area in our house yard. My father made an incision in the lower part of the leg near the hoof and stretched out a tendon through which a lifting bar of wood was inserted. This bar had to support the weight of the hog when hung up, and therefore was cured hickory. Each hog was dragged individually, by mule. Half of the hog was lowered into the scalding water and rotated several times. The other half was treated the same way. The hair was then scraped off with a large knife. Most of the hair came out.

The hog now had a body that was mostly free of hair. A hog weighing several hundred pounds required three men to lift and hang. The head was then removed and the body gutted down the belly. The liver, maw, and other parts were saved and cooked to be used later. The body was dismembered, hams and some belly slabs prepared for smoking, and other parts for salting down. Excess fat was trimmed and cooked in the cast iron wash pot. This resulted in lard, which when cooled solidified and was stored in large tin containers. The remains were cracklings and could be used in making corn bread.

I don't remember cutting pork chops, therefore I believe the loins were used in making sausage. All the meat was cut away from the backbone and ground in a small hand-cranked grinder. After grinding, the grinder had a tube reducer attached to the output. The ground meat was fed through again and stuffed in casings, which had been purchased earlier. The backbone was a favorite of all. Each got some and usually cooked it in a large pot of rice.

We had a small building without a floor that was the smokehouse. Hams, sausages, and bacon slabs were hung from a pole rack. A small smoldering fire was kept going for weeks while the meat cured. All other meat was salted down and packed in a chest of pure salt. When there was no smoke coming through the rafters of the smokehouse, we knew the fire needed attending.

As the winter weather waned, the planting season was upon us. A flat bed about four to five feet wide and 100 or more feet long was prepared and smoothed. I remember a bag of seeds, about 25 pounds, that looked like the little black basil seed we now know. These seeds were sowed on the bed and very lightly raked to cover. The planting was timed so as to avoid frost when the plants came up. One time a very thin gauze-like white material was spread over the entire bed. I assume this was to help protect from expected frost. On Daniel Island we had a jump of about one to two weeks on the planting season elsewhere around Charleston. This was due to the location of the two rivers, the Cooper and the Wando, to each side of the island. The water temperature gave this advantage.

As the seeds were growing into small cabbage plants the planting fields were being prepared. At this time the only tractor was an all-metal "Farmall" brand. It was very slow and had metal cleats on the back wheels. The ground had to be turned with plows. The plow was about eight inches wide and dug six to eight inches deep. This was a one horse or mule plow. Usually two, three, and four plows followed each other. You can imagine how long it took to make a round when the speed was a slow step for the plowman.

The next step was to form beds and furoughs. Now the plowman used a center plow which ploughed a furrough, and on the round trip the reverse made one bed and one half of the other. Again, this was very slow. At one time we had as many as seven to nine mules.

Time to plant but we want the plants equidistant apart to allow for large head growth but not to waste planting space. A roller drum is constructed of wooden ends with an axle. The outer rim of the drum is also wood, about six feet long and two feet in diameter. On the drum surface one inch by one inch slats are mounted approximately one foot apart or whatever plant spacing is wanted. This drum is pulled by a mule with the driver walking behind so as not to press the beds. The one-inch bars leave a marking in two beds at a time. Again, very slow.

Cabbage planting begins. The small cabbage plants are pulled from the bed. The planting labor was usually the women. They wore an apron with a pocket for carrying a handful of plants. Each person had a round implement about 10 inches long with one end made of iron about one-and-a-half inches in diameter. A hole was punched in the grove on the bed, a plant inserted, and then the dirt was slapped with the implement to pack the root. This required a lot of walking while in a stoop.

As the cabbage plant began maturing, plowing had to be done. First fertilizer was dropped in the furrows from a mechanical spreader, usually covering about four furrows. I believe this was a two-mule operation. A one-mule center plow down each furrow would plow up any weeds and throw the fertilizer up around the plants.

In the meantime, other ground was being prepared for potato planting. The same process of plowing the ground to cover and soften the soil was used. I don't remember whether the potatoes were planted before harvesting the cabbage or not.

To harvest the cabbage, again the labor was mostly women. A cart pulled by a mule would move a few steps forward and stop. This cart had been lined with burlap bags to lessen the damage to a head of cabbage as it was tossed as an underhanded basketball shot. The women had knives about two feet long. One swipe to remove the head from the earth and one swipe to trim the head of unwanted leaves. When filled this cart would move out to Bellinger Island packing shed. The cabbage heads were put in a circular crate about two feet high. A lid was wired down on the crate and it was ready for shipping. The crates were smaller at the bottom tapering outward toward the top. These crates were loaded on a boat or barge at the pier. The boat was the *Thelma*, owned by Captain Thelling and named for his wife, so the story goes. The barge was towed or pushed as the tide would allow, by a small tugboat named the *Do Do*, also owned by captain Thelling. At the American Fruit Growers pier in Charleston, the crates of cabbage were packed in railroad cars. When the car was loaded, blocks of ice were crushed and sprayed over the crates before closing the doors. I don't know what market they went to.

Some time while this was going on the potato fields were being prepared for planting potatoes. The main potato was a "cobbler," mostly grown in the state of

Maine. I remember one year we planted the "green mountain potato." This potato was longer and had a smoother skin.

The seed potato was cut in sections so that each section had at least one eye. These seeds were treated in a solution to prevent underground rodents from eating the seed. For planting, a hopper-like planter with rotating pins that picked up a seed would cover at least two beds. Under and in front of the hopper was a small v-shaped plow that plowed a trench three to four inches deep into which a seed was dropped. Two small plows followed behind on each bed throwing dirt over the seeds.

In the meantime, the cabbage fields were plowed under and corn planted. During this time several litters of pigs were appearing. When the males were old enough to weigh about 20 pounds, my dad castrated them. I helped hold them down for this operation. I asked why, and his answer was that as barrows they would grow into bigger hogs. I do not know if this was the practice at all farms or who the other surgeons were.

During the potato growing season, the weeds were plowed and fertilizer applied to the potatoes as with the cabbage. Now the used cabbage fields had to be prepared for another crop. A disk harrow was the best implement to slice up the old cabbage and roots. Again the fields were plowed to turn over the soil and cover any vegetation. Beds were again prepared. This time corn is planted. It takes a lot of corn to feed the mules and hogs for a year.

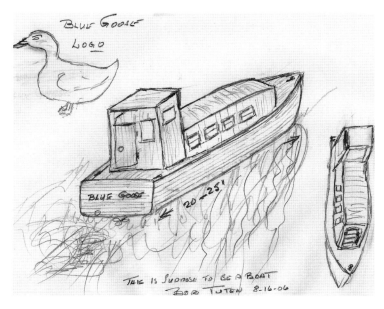

The Blue Goose was a small boat owned by the American Fruit Growers that provided transportation from Mitchell Pier to Charleston's South Street Warf. (Courtesy Bob Tuten.)

Bob Tuten is seen here in 1941, shortly after he left Daniel Island. He had lived on the island since 1935. His home was close to the present-day Bishop England High School and can be seen on maps of Daniel Island as early as 1918. (Courtesy Bob Tuten.)

Many times the potato plants had to be sprayed with a lime dust because of potato bugs. I remember seeing the sprayer going late in the afternoon and as long as there was enough daylight to see. The wind was calm at this time and the spraying more effective. During the growing season we would scratch under the plants and pick golf-ball size potatoes, then recover the base. I'm sure a lot of the laborers did the same.

Time for potato harvesting in mid to late May. A potato plow, pulled by two mules, has a deep runner and large wings to spread the potatoes over the dirt. Women, children, everybody picks up potatoes. As the potato beds are exposed my dad would mark off sections and assign to a person or persons. He used stakes to give each one or groups equal share. One row was assigned as the staging row to simplify the loading and hauling operation. As each staging row was finished he would tally up the containers for each person. Picking up was usually in a small crate, which was dumped into a barrel or some years into burlap bags. As there was only one truck on the island, a couple of trucks with owners and drivers were brought over on a barge each year. One of these truck owners was my father's nephew. He would stay with us, as there was nowhere to stay. He had a new Ford truck that was bought stripped. By this I mean a hood covered the engine, and there was a windshield. All body parts stopped at the windshield. From there to the back was an exposed gas tank and nothing but chassis. He built a seat over the gas tank and a platform over the chassis. If I had to guess the price I would say he bought it for under $500. Gas was 18¢ a gallon. There was a gas pump near the general store but this was for the two company vehicles and tractor. A handle was for pumping gas up to a glass 10-gallon cylinder. Gas for the visitors was brought over (probably on the mail boat) in 55-gallon drums. A drum was brought to our house and mounted on a bench higher than the truck gas tank. A siphon hose was used to fill the truck tank.

For my father's farm the truck would haul the potatoes to Bellinger Island packing shed for grading, bagging, and shipping. They would haul to other farms also. Some kind of old vehicle engine turned the grader. One or two people would sit along the belt and remove damaged potatoes. The potatoes were graded as #1, #2, #3, and waste. One year the market was so good even the #3s sold. Usually only the #1 and #2 were shipped. All leftovers were hauled to a field and dumped for the hogs. All could not be consumed; therefore, there was a lot of rotting. This was eventually plowed under to get rid of the stench.

When the season was frost free we began planting a garden. We grew many kinds of vegetables. Always a lot of tomatoes because this was a main canning product. My mother would can many quarts of tomatoes to last throughout the winter. Other vegetables were beans, peas, squash, cucumbers, watermelons, cantaloupes, and sweet potatoes. The sweet potato was a main item grown by the laborers. From a few seed potatoes would grow many vines. These vines were cut into sections about one foot long. The vine was laid on the bed and about midpoint pushed into the soft dirt of a bed. Each vine would produce many potatoes. To keep the sweet potato all year a shallow hole was dug and a layer of pine straw added. Sweet potatoes would be piled in a mound about three feet high. This mound was covered with pine straw and a six- to eight-inch layer of dirt. To get the potatoes during the winter a small hole was dug at the base of the potato bank and the potatoes pulled out. The hole was then covered until another need for potatoes. The Irish potato was stored in a dark house with a ground floor and no light source. The sweet potato was a main source of food for the laborers. They grew many and ate them year-round.

With the end of potato harvesting the fields were plowed and oats or more corn were planted. Some places a cover crop was planted. Later in the year the corn was harvested. A cart and driver would stay ahead of several people breaking the ears from the stalk and tossing them into the cart. I don't remember if the corn ear was shucked at that time or later. However, the huge pile of corn in the barn was without shuck. There was enough planted and picked to feed the mules and the hogs through the seasons. Also the chickens. We had many.

The oats were mowed with a mower machine. This machine looked like a huge hedge trimmer mounted to the side of two wheels where the driver sat to drive the mules. After lying in the field for a while to dry, the oats were raked into piles with a long tooth rake pulled by a mule. The next step was to load the oats on a cart that had been oversized with wings. Adjacent to the barnyard the oats were shocked into large stacks around a pole.

Some of the cover crops, usually a vine like kudzu, were mowed and stacked as hay. But most of it was cut in with a disc harrow to enrich the soil.

There was a blacksmith shop on the island and it was very much in use. It was located near the intersection of Daniel Island Drive and Seven Farms Drive on the southeast corner. The deep-well pump was across Seven Farms Drive at the northeast corner. Only a narrow road of about 20 feet separated them. It was nothing but a shack. I recall a name of "Blake" as possibly the black smithy. This could be his given name or surname or could be entirely wrong.

There was a firing area with a bellows. He let me turn the handle forcing air to the fire. Strangely this fire was of coal, which I had not seen before. I asked why not wood for the fire. He said that coal burned hotter to heat the metal. While the mules did not have shoes, I do believe the horses of the managers had shoes. The rims around the carts, about five feet in diameter, would wear through and had to be repaired. Also broken parts to plows and later tractors. In the blacksmith shop area there were a lot of discarded metal parts from plows. That is if the Japanese didn't get it all. The bridge had been completed over the creek, and the Japanese brought in a truck and hauled away all the scrap iron. We may have given it to them but I believe we sold it.

Now was the time to shoot rabbits. A section about 50 feet wide would be cut on each side. As the uncut part got narrower the rabbits would run for cover. I had a single-shot 20 gauge bolt action shotgun that my father bought me one Christmas. A box of 25 shells cost 75¢. The laborers would pay me 15¢ for a rabbit. Also, blackbirds at 1¢ each. If I didn't get reckless shooting I could keep myself in shells for my gun. During this time of getting the gun I decided I wanted a guitar. I ordered one through Sears for $3.50. One week later my progress of playing the guitar led me to sell it.

Late in the fall after most of the plowing-under of the cover crop and harvesting the oats, we were nearing hog killing time again. There was still some work to do. All the fields had many ditches. Water from the fields was trenched by water furrough across the beds to a ditch. By late fall these ditches had grown six to eight feet high and the ditch accumulated runoff sand. Laborers chopped down the growth, and burning it took weeks. Then the ditches were retrenched or cleaned out. While walking home from school, I would detour and walk down a cleaned ditch. In a few areas I would find sassafras roots in the side of the ditch. My father liked sassafras tea so I would pull a few roots and bring home a pocket full.

One laborer family, Jim and Rosa Sanders, lived just west of us across a small wetland. They had several children but Isaac was my age, and my buddy. His dad built a boat about 10 feet long and kept it in the creek directly west on the Cooper River. A small pier was built out of sticks and driftwood boards. This is where he and I and my brothers and his brothers would swim when the tide came in. No bathing attire required. Isaac's dad also could knit shrimp nets. We went fishing but had to catch our shrimp first. Sometimes we could get a few on the river's edge. The best places were holes in the small creeks before the tide would flood the area. We would drag the boat across the beach area into these creeks. One or two casts with the net usually produced a couple dozen shrimp, enough for one fishing day. We fished the bottom and caught croaker, whiting, spots, and sea trout, also small sharks. Isaac and his family liked to eat the shark. We didn't.

Larger homes were provided to the white farm managers, who oversaw the operations on one of the seven named farms. These homes were based on a four-room design, and had two interior fireplaces. This house was abandoned in 1941 when the Tuten family moved away from Daniel Island and razed in 1949 when Guggenheim cleared many of the old buildings not needed to support his cattle ranch. The fireplace foundations remain today. (Courtesy Bob Tuten.)

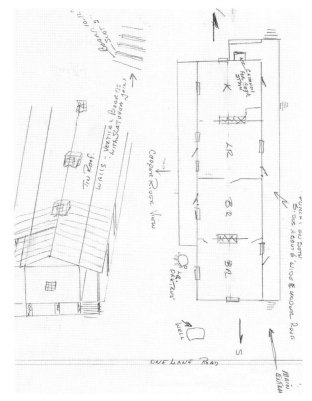

One May during a flood tide the wetland to the river looked like the river was almost at our back door. Isaac and I, with my 20-gauge shotgun and my dog Smokey, went marsh-hen hunting. As we paddled the marsh grass, Smokey swam ahead and would search the small islands. The marsh hens swam out and I got ten that day. When my father came in from the fields that Friday afternoon he had to go next day. For some reason Smokey didn't come with us. The results, one marsh hen.

If we had four people we could always get up a ball game. Part of the wetland was a flat clean sandy area when the tide was out. This was our ballpark. Any old piece of lumber (driftwood) was a bat. We could find on the river's beach an old tennis ball or a small sponge ball. We usually ended up using one half of a ball. This was more interesting. You could do crazy things with only one half of a ball. You either struck out, or if you hit the ball, the best method of getting you out was to hit you with the ball. Therefore, no first baseman was needed. Pick off was easy too.

Isaac and I spent hours perfecting a wooden crotch for a slingshot handle. Rubber strips were cut from any old tire tube we could find. This piece of rubber was kept as a valuable piece of property. Small rubber strips were cut and tied to the crotch and to an old shoe tongue. For ammo the best was an old plow point broken into slugs. We used small rocks also, from the beach. We were both good shots. A bird at 30 to 40 feet didn't stand a chance. Isaac would clean the birds and take them home to fry.

When the tide was in we swam in the creek near the river to the west. No clothes required. Sometimes we would go to the pier on Bellinger Island to swim. If we didn't have bathing trunks, no problem—we improvised. It was unheard of to swim in your underwear because we wore bvd's. These were the type made in one piece with short legs and no sleeves. That would have been too embarrassing. Instead, we found burlap potato sacks, cut the bottom corners for leg holes and a piece of wire or nail to pin the waist. Sometimes we had to use a piece of the sack and put it on as a baby diaper. Needless to say we were all dressed alike. My brother, who was four years younger, would climb the highest piling and plunge into the creek.

My father and my uncle Eddie of Scott farm would sometimes hunt quail. My dog Smokey was supposed to be a bird dog but he was poorly trained and would flush the birds instead of pointing. We didn't get too many quail as a result.

Following this period, two tractors were incorporated into the farming. One large John Deere with huge tires could pull two plow blades, the equivalent of four or five standard one-mule plows. Also the speed was at least five times greater than that of a mule. Therefore this one tractor could do the work of about 25 plows. The other tractor was a John Deer with plows rigged forward of the driver and behind the tractor. These plow blades were V-shaped to throw dirt in both directions. As many as three beds or rows of cabbage, corn, or potatoes could be plowed at a time. The tractor and one driver would take the place of as many as 15 to 20 people. These tractors were used throughout the farms.

Fuel for cars and tractors on Daniel Island was stored in above-ground tanks such as this one near the Beresford Creek Golf Course. Fuel was transported to the island by boat until the Beresford Creek bridges were built in 1939.

During that time, the tenants asked for all the old magazines and newspapers that we had. With a mixing of flour and water, they papered the interior of their houses. They were probably warmer than ours were.

The Mail Boat went from Cainhoy, to Mitchell Pier, and then to Charleston. It cost 15¢ to ride one way. The boat would also stop at Pole Grove Pier or Acme Pier if one waved a handkerchief to flag the boat down. A small post office was located in the Mitchell Pier complex, and was called Remleys Point. Postcards were 1¢, and a letter could be sent for 3¢.

Every farm had a cow and we bought 75 pounds of ice about every five days for 75¢ that came from Charleston to Mitchell Pier by the mail boat. Our milk was kept cool in the ice chest and the cream skimmed. A one-quart jar about two-thirds full of cream, shaken lightly for about 30 minutes, would produce about half a pound of butter. One of my jobs.

There was no electricity anywhere on the island. We only had one thing electric, a Zenith radio that had about five different batteries. I remember hurrying from playing to get home to listen to *The Lone Ranger*. It was a serial and I had to know what happened next. Another favorite show was *Fibber McGee & Molly*. Broadcasters were WCSC and WTMA in Charleston. Any other reception was high-power stations in New Orleans, Nashville, and Pittsburgh. The batteries didn't last too long. When they started to fade we could only listen to H. V. Keltenborn with the war news as Hitler was invading European countries.

Most of our clothes were bought through the Sears catalog. Any item wrong size or color could be returned postage free. Very few clothes were ironed since we were farmers. To iron those that needed it my mother had two choices. She had what was known as a gas iron. This gadget had a small tank about the size of a tennis ball. In this tank she poured a small amount of white gasoline and with a small hand pump pressurized the gas tank. White gas contained less impurities to reduce the clogging of jets. She would then open the jets and light with a match. Sometimes she would have to heat heavy metal irons on the stove when the gas iron didn't work.

I believe we must have bought our ice chest through Sears because I had this huge cardboard box on the porch where my dog Smokey stayed. That is the only explanation I have for such a box. Smokey went to school with me every day and stayed until I came home. This box was also my refuge for sulking!

We bought very little at the big store. Mostly small items, when we needed them, such as matches for 1¢ a box or 5¢ for a strike-anywhere large box, commonly known as kitchen matches. Sugar sometimes, I believe it was about 15¢ a pound. A six-ounce bottle of Coca-Cola was 6¢. Bologna was 15 to 20¢ per pound. Sometimes for school lunch, when there were no leftovers from the night before, mother gave me a dime and at recess I would go to the store and buy a piece of bologna, approximately a quarter pound for a nickel. Then with the other nickel I'd buy macaroon crackers at two for 1¢. Water was the only drink at school. Soft drinks were too expensive. Besides, there was a limited choice. A six-ounce Coca-Cola, or the frosted heavy glass bottle by Coca-Cola, Orange Crush, grape, or strawberry. A competitor was a 12-ounce RC Cola. For cigarettes, a package of Target tobacco for roll-your-own was 12¢. For the pipe smokers, and many of the workers' wives smoked pipes, a package of George Washington pipe tobacco was also 12¢. My dad smoked cigarettes and sometimes a pipe. His choice was Prince Albert in a red tin can, about 15¢. He rolled his own. I was amazed how he could roll the fine-cut tobacco in a small tissue.

On other occasions, when the local bosses of the American Fruit Company were over they had noon dinner at the superintendent's house. My aunt would invite me to come home with her children and have dinner also. One thing I remember is how discretely each of them tucked 15¢ under their plate after the meal was over. This evidently was the established price for the meal. They only came during the busy time, summer. Vegetables were plentiful and my aunt cooked the best cornbread sticks I've ever eaten. I cook them today out of ready-mix.

The *Blue Goose* boat was a motor launch approximately 20 to 25 feet long. The front was enclosed with a bench on either side. Seating for eight to ten people. The engine room and steering cabin rose above the front. No cargo. Every Thursday afternoon and sometimes in the night the worksheet from each farm was delivered to the superintendent. Every Friday morning the payroll sheets were taken on the

A blacksmith shop was located at the present-day site of the Holy Cross Episcopal Church at the intersection of Daniel Island Drive and Seven Farms Road. This shop repaired the many farm implements, carts, and wagons used in truck farming. In 1939, a Japanese company purchased much of the excess metal that was on the site. The lumber from this shop was subsequently used to construct the fence and gate at the entrance to Simmons Cemetery. (Courtesy Brockington and Associates.)

This photograph was taken by Bob Tuten from his home on Daniel Island in the summer of 1938. It shows the USS Dunlap and the USS Fanning tied up for repairs at the Charleston Naval Base. The two modified Mahan-class destroyers shared a connection with Daniel Island when they took part in Lt. Col. Jimmy Doolittle's raid on Tokyo in April 1942, soon after U.S. entry in World War II. Doolittle later became a frequent guest of Harry Guggenheim on Daniel Island. The Dunlap escorted the USS Enterprise near Pearl Harbor the day the carrier left Hawaii to rendezvous with the USS Hornet, which held Doolittle's aircraft. The Fanning was an escort of the Hornet task force that sailed within 600 miles of the Japanese coast. The ships saw further action together in raids against Japanese oil production facilities in Sumatra and Java, and in the battle for Iwo Jima.

boat to Charleston. That afternoon the wages were brought back and delivered to each farm in the form of cash in envelopes. The island mechanic was also the boat captain. He let me steer the boat sometimes. He always had a revolver strapped to his side when returning to the boat in Charleston.

Usually the last Saturday in the month, when the managers were paid by check, the boat would take those wanting to go shopping to Charleston and return that afternoon. This is when we did our major grocery shopping. A major grocery store was Heinsons on East Bay just a few hundred yards from the American Fruit Growers pier. Prior to 1939, we garaged our car in a tin building behind the grocery store. Sometimes we would drive to Colleton County near Yemassee to visit. The boat would meet us on a Sunday afternoon for transportation back to Daniel Island. From our house to the boat at Mitchell and back the superintendent or his sons would drive us in the only car on the island, a model-A Ford. I remember the main part of town was Calhoun Street at King Street. Then south on King, a very narrow street with a trolley track down the middle. During that time my dad was interested in listening to Mr. Maybank speak on the steps of the custom house, for mayor of Charleston. He couldn't vote because we were in Berkeley County.

This portrait shows Harry Frank Guggenheim in the early 1960s. (Courtesy Harry Frank Guggenheim Foundation.)

9. THE GUGGENHEIM ERA

American Fruit Growers consolidated operations on the farms in the early 1940s as the war and changing market conditions made profitable operations a challenge. By 1943, there were only three farm managers on the island, with Bob Tuten and his family moving off in 1941 and his brother moving off in 1942. Aerial photography of the island from 1949, as well as the inventory of the island conducted in mid-1946 show that only one pier remained in use and most of the warehouses from the truck-farming days were gone. At the end of 1944, the company sought a buyer for the operation. On May 21, 1945, John F. Maybank, who was the brother of the governor of South Carolina and a stockholder of American Fruit Growers, purchased the land and associated buildings and the pier for $60,000. Maybank continued farming operations on the island in 1945, operating seven farms: Mitchell, Pole Grove, Bard, Center, Acme, Scott, and Bridge. On May 17, 1946, Harry Frank Guggenheim purchased the Maybank farm for $75,000. This land included 2,938 acres, of which 1,000 were arable. The remaining nearly 2,000 acres were marsh and forested wetlands.

Guggenheim's purchase of the lower two thirds of Daniel Island did not come as a surprise to most Charlestonians. The Guggenheims had a deepening relationship with Charleston and the Lowcountry by the mid 1940s. Solomon Guggenheim, Harry Guggenheim's uncle, had purchased a 12,000-acre plantation south of Walterboro named "Big Survey" in the 1920s. Big Survey took its name from the art world, where "surveys" were samplings of an artist's work or a display of many artists' work representing a particular genre. The Big Survey plantation was used as a hunting preserve in its early years and then a well-respected stable that produced race horses that ran at tracks in Florida, Maryland, New Jersey, and New York under the care of Barbara Guggenheim-Obre, one of Solomon's three daughters. Guggenheim also purchased the Roper House on Charleston's High Battery from the Sieglings family in 1929 and was a winter guest in Charleston in the 1930s. Another of Harry Guggenheim's uncles, Robert, purchased a 1,700-acre plantation called Poco Sabo, meaning "little unknown," on the Ashepoo River, which he held until 1971.

The Cain Hoy Plantation House is pictured shortly after its completion in 1936. Guggenheim spent over $250,000 to have the house built and equipped it with a water-filtration system and an electrical generator to provide light and power for the stove. Large rows of live oaks mark the main road of the 1790s Hartford Plantation that previously occupied the site. (Courtesy Harry Frank Guggenheim Foundation.)

Cain Hoy Plantation

Harry Guggenheim's first purchase of land in the Daniel Island area occurred in 1935. The low land prices and the collapse of the timber industry following the Great Depression made large tracts of land readily available. Guggenheim, like his counterparts in many of the great and powerful families of the north, continued looking for land throughout the Depression for hunting preserves. He had just returned to the United States from Cuba, where he had been the U.S. ambassador from 1931 to 1933. His familiarity with the Lowcountry, spurred in part by his association with Big Survey, made the South Carolina coast a natural choice for him. One of his lawyers, Paul Barringer, had a brother Victor who was a forester for the Sumter Hardwood Company in Sumter, South Carolina. Victor Barringer, along with Frank Traver, the operations manager at Sumter Hardwood, had information about what land was available for purchase in the Lowcountry. They worked on behalf of Guggenheim for several years, eventually accumulating over 10,000 acres that Guggenheim purchased in 1935 and named the Cain Hoy plantation. They chose this name due to the plantation's proximity to the town of Cainhoy and consistently used the two-word spelling. The lands had originally been granted to some of the earliest landowners in Charleston, including Beresford and Smith, and included the former Hartford Plantation site, which was a working plantation in the late 1790s just south of Flagg's Creek on the Cooper River.

One of Guggenheim's first orders of business was to build a large house on the site to serve as both a retreat for his family and, perhaps more importantly, as a hunting lodge for him and his guests. The lodge was completed at a cost of over $250,000 in late 1936, and it became one of the centers of Guggenheim's social life until his death in 1971. He was a frequent visitor to Charleston, and the locals considered him a "winter resident of the Lowcountry." The Guggenheims kept a guest book of the visitors to the lodge, and Peter

Harry Guggenheim approached the conversion of Daniel Island from a vegetable farm to a cattle ranch with the same attention to detail and business savvy that were the hallmarks of all his ventures. This inventory, taken one year after he acquired the southern two-thirds of the island, provides an interesting view into both what he purchased and the pace at which he was adding livestock to his ranch. (Courtesy Library of Congress.)

Lawson-Johnston has kept up that tradition since he inherited the estate in 1971. There were hunting parties twice a year, typically in December and February, as well as visits by family during the Christmas holiday season.

Shortly after World War II ended, Guggenheim began to invite a group he called the "generals" to the plantation to hunt turkey and quail. General James Doolittle, whom Guggenheim had met and supported in the late 1920s, was one of the most frequent guests for over 20 years and assumed responsibility for coordinating this group by telegram and letter. The group included Generals Doolittle, Hoyt Vandenberg, Pat Partridge, Hank Everest, Nat Twining, Pete Quesada, Vive Admiral Emory Land, and Senator Harry Byrd.

During the generals' visits, the morning would be dedicated to turkey hunting on the main plantation grounds. During the afternoon, quail and dove were hunted on Daniel Island. "Turkey" Tucker lived on the plantation from 1940 until his death in 1957 and was responsible for the care of the hunting dogs as well as for tending to the wild turkeys on the plantation, and for raising quail that were to be released at various locations on Daniel Island thus establishing a "natural" population that could be hunted. His

In 1947, Guggenheim purchased an 18-foot Lyman Islander similar to this one. This was in addition to the 25-foot ChrisCraft Clipper he had purchased in November 1936. The shallow draft of the Islander allowed Guggenheim access to the smaller creeks and marshes of Daniel Island for hunting further afield from the main Cain Hoy plantation. (Courtesy Library of Congress.)

Pictured are Guggenheim, Dark Star, and jockey Henry Moreno in the winners circle at Churchill Downs following Dark Star's victory in the 79th running of the Kentucky Derby in 1953. Bred and raised at Cain Hoy Stables, Dark Star was the only horse ever to beat Hall of Famer Native Dancer, owned by Alfred Vanderbilt. (Courtesy Library of Congress.)

knowledge of the wild turkey, as well as its habits and habitats, was invaluable to the success of the parties. A brass plaque, signed by those who frequently hunted under his supervision, hangs on the front of Cain Hoy plantation today. In 1962, Cain Hoy was granted status as a private hunting preserve. Legislation had been passed to limit turkey hunting season to the fall unless more than 10,000 acres were held by an owner. This was to ensure that wild turkey flocks, which were being decimated by overhunting, remained viable. The private preserve designation allowed turkey shoots to continue in both the fall and the spring on Cain Hoy.

Cain Hoy plantation was far more than a rich northerner's playground. Guggenheim operated a large and successful timber operation there. He sought expert advice on how to best grow southern pine from state agricultural organizations, and funded the Coastal Lumber Corporation, which was run and owned by Victor Barringer. Guggenheim's relationship with Barringer, formed as land was acquired for Cain Hoy, was typical of how he trusted people who helped him and rewarded hard work and dedication. Barringer and Coastal Lumber had exclusive logging rights on Cain Hoy, and timber was cut and milled on the plantation and sent by barge to Charleston. Barringer remained

Harry Guggenheim had a deep belief in the future of aviation, thanks to his time as a naval aviator in World War I. He convinced his father, Daniel, to invest in the fledgling industry and fund efforts to make aviation safer. This was accomplished by the establishment of the Daniel and Florence Guggenheim Foundation. In this 1926 meeting of the foundation's board, Harry (back row, second from right) is seen with his lifelong friend Charles Lindbergh (back row, third from right) along with Orville Wright (first row, to the left). (Courtesy Library of Congress.)

a trusted advisor in all potential additional land acquisitions that Guggenheim considered in the Lowcountry, including the purchase of lower Daniel Island in 1946 and the remainder of the island, called the Furman Track, in 1955.

A second line of business that Harry Guggenheim opened in South Carolina was the breeding of thoroughbred race horses. Cain Hoy Stables were established in the mid-1940s. Guggenheim sought out the best breeders in the United States for advice and support. These efforts resulted in a stable that became recognized as one of the country's best by the mid-1960s. Today several of the thoroughbred lines he created are still sought after for stud. His crowning achievement occurred in 1953, when Dark Star won the Kentucky Derby, beating Native Dancer, who was owned by Alfred Vanderbilt, by less than a body length. In 1959 the stable won more prize money than any other stable in the country, and Bald Eagle won the International at Laurel, Maryland. Bald Eagle won this race again in 1960 and remains the only horse to have won it twice. In 1963, Guggenheim was named breeder of the year in England for breeding Ragusa. Ack Ack was the last horse bred and raced by Guggenheim, and he won the Aqueduct in 1969. However, by 1969 Guggenheim was diagnosed with prostate cancer, and he began to sell off the Cain Hoy horses to other stables. By the end of 1969, Cain Hoy Stables was effectively out of business. In 1971, Ack Ack was sold by the estate but went on to be named 1971 thoroughbred horse of the year and in 1986 was induced into the thoroughbred hall of fame.

The Visitors to Cain Hoy

The most notable visitors to Cain Hoy included James H. "Jimmy" Doolittle and Charles Lindbergh, both famous aviation pioneers who shared Guggenheim's passion for promoting advances in flight. They had met as a part of their association with the Daniel Guggenheim Fund for the Promotion of Aeronautics, which was established in 1926. This fund greatly furthered

Guggenheim, as president of the Guggenheim Foundation, provided sponsorship for much of the pioneering research of Dr. Robert H. Goddard, upon which all modern rocket and jet propulsion developments are based. Guggenheim visited Goddard at Roswell, New Mexico, in September 1935. Pictured are, from left to right: Albert Kisk, Goddard's brother-in-law and machinist; Guggenheim; Dr. Robert Goddard; Charles Lindbergh; Nils Ljungquist, machinist; and Charles Mansur, welder. (Courtesy Harry Frank Guggenheim Foundation.)

Pictured is Vice Admiral John S. McCain, the deputy chief of naval air operations, congratulating Commander Harry Frank Guggenheim on becoming the commanding officer at the commissioning of Mercer Field near Trenton, New Jersey. To the right is Captain Newton H. White Jr., commanding officer at the U.S. Naval Air Station Floyd Bennet Field. (Courtesy Harry Frank Guggenheim Foundation.)

the fledgling aviation industry and helped to establish schools of aeronautical engineering across the country. It also supported a Safe Aircraft Competition to encourage aerodynamic safety without loss of aircraft efficiency.

James H. Doolittle

Born December 16, 1896 in Alameda, California, James H. "Jimmy" Doolittle joined the U.S. Army in October 1917 as a flying cadet and was commissioned a second lieutenant in the Signal Corps Aviation Section on March 11, 1918. During the war, he served as a flight leader and gunnery instructor. After the war, he remained in the army and became one of the most famous pilots in the 1920s and 1930s. In September 1922, he completed the first cross-country flight, from Pablo Beach, Florida to Rockwell Field in San Diego, California in 21 hours and 19 minutes. He was a test pilot and aeronautical engineer in 1923, and in June 1924 he received a masters in aeronautics from MIT. He raced airplanes and set speed records for propeller-driven aircraft in 1925 and 1926.

During the late 1920s, the Daniel and Florence Guggenheim Foundation dedicated itself to the improvement of rocketry, aviation, and aviation technology. Harry Guggenheim was present at many of Doolittle's races, and was on hand to observe perhaps Doolittle's greatest contribution to aviation development. On September 14, 1929, he became the first person to fly totally by instruments. With the cockpit canopy completely covered, he took off, flew 10 miles, and landed safely without any visual references. In the 1930s, Doolittle was working with Shell Oil Company to produce a special high-octane fuel needed to power high performance aircraft, including the combat aircraft that would eventually be built for World War II.

In January 1942, Doolittle volunteered to lead what would become known as "The Doolittle Raid" on Tokyo, a daring retaliation for the bombing of Pearl Harbor just weeks before. His knowledge of aerodynamics, flying, and engineering, as well as a lifetime of flying firsts made him the ideal choice for such a task. On April 2, the USS *Hornet* left Alameda, California with 16 Army Air Force B-25 Mitchell bombers on its flight deck. Never before

Guggenheim served in both World War I and World War II and was awarded the Asiatic-Pacific Campaign Ribbon for action against the Japanese in Niyako-Shima on June 7, 1944. He is pictured heading to the flight deck aboard the USS Nehemntha Bay *in June 1944. (Courtesy Harry Frank Guggenheim Foundation.)*

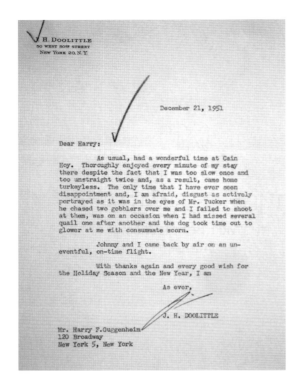

December 21, 1951

Dear Harry:

As usual, had a wonderful time at Cain Hoy. Thoroughly enjoyed every minute of my stay there despite the fact that I was too slow once and too unstraight twice and, as a result, came home turkeyless. The only time that I have ever seen disappointment and, I am afraid, disgust as actively portrayed as it was in the eyes of Mr. Tucker when he chased two gobblers over me and I failed to shoot at them, was on an occasion when I had missed several quail one after another and the dog took time out to glower at me with consummate scorn.

Johnny and I came back by air on an uneventful, on-time flight.

With thanks again and every good wish for the Holiday Season and the New Year, I am

As ever,

J. H. DOOLITTLE

Mr. Harry F. Guggenheim
120 Broadway
New York 5, New York

General Doolittle was one of the most frequent visitors to Cain Hoy for almost 20 years. He arranged for the generals to attend annual hunting parties on the plantation and Daniel Island during the Christmas season. Typically, turkey were hunted in the morning on the main plantation grounds, and quail and dove were hunted on Daniel Island during the afternoon. (Courtesy Library of Congress.)

had army bombers been launched from a Navy carrier with a full load of fuel and bombs. On April 16, with the *Hornet* 600 miles from the Japanese coast, Doolittle was the first plane off, having only 467 feet of runway to get his B-25 into the air. Within hours, U.S. forces had bombed Tokyo, Nagoya, Osaka, Kobe, and Yokahama. This raid, while causing minimal damage, was a great morale booster for the American people, and also forced the Japanese military to keep significant numbers of aircraft and warships closer to the homeland instead of deploying them in other battles in the Pacific theater. Lt. Col. Jimmy Doolittle earned the Congressional Medal of Honor for his role in leading the mission.

Charles Lindbergh

Born February 4, 1902 in Detroit, Charles Augustus Lindbergh grew up on a farm near Little Falls, Minnesota. His father served as a U.S. congressman from Minnesota from 1907 to 1917. Lindbergh gained sudden great international fame as the first pilot to fly solo and non-stop across the

Atlantic Ocean, flying from New York to Paris on May 20 to May 21, 1927 in his single-engine aircraft *The Spirit of St. Louis.* Before Lindbergh left for Paris, Guggenheim visited him at Curtiss Field and told him "when you get back from your flight, look me up." Guggenheim later admitted he didn't think there was much chance Lindbergh would survive the trip.

Upon his return, Lindbergh remembered Guggenheim's invitation and did call. The two pilots soon forged a friendship that would span their lifetimes and would profoundly affect the development of commercial aviation in the United States. Lindbergh, under the sponsorship of the Daniel Guggenheim Fund for the Promotion of Aeronautics, embarked on a three-month tour of the United States. Flying the *Spirit of St. Louis,* he touched down in 49 states, visited 92 cities, gave 147 speeches, and rode 1,290 miles in parades. Lindbergh was seen by millions of people as he flew around the country, and overnight the use of airmail increased and confidence in the safety of air travel grew.

In 1929, Lindbergh became interested in the work of rocket pioneer Robert Goddard. The following year, Lindbergh helped Goddard secure his first endowment from the Guggenheim Fund, which allowed Goddard to

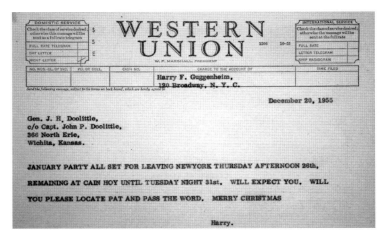

Until the early 1960s, telegrams were Guggenheim's preferred method of communication when a message had to be delivered quickly and accurately. The Christmas season in 1955–1956 was a busy time at Cain Hoy. The generals had been guests for five days in early December, and Guggenheim's daughter Joan and her husband spent Christmas there. Another hunting party stayed into the new year, and the three generals who had not attended the hunt in December were at Cain Hoy at the end of January. (Courtesy Library of Congress.)

The ties that were formed between General Doolittle (left), Charles Lindbergh (right), and Harry Guggenheim (center) in the pioneering days of aviation led to a lifelong friendship among the men. This gathering was part of a later series of meetings they held to forge a process to understand human relationships and find the roots of aggression and dominance. (Courtesy Harry Frank Guggenheim Foundation.)

expand his independent research and development. Lindbergh remained a key supporter and advocate of Goddard's work throughout his life, which led to the development of missiles, satellites, and space travel.

Lindbergh and Guggenheim remained close throughout their lifetimes, but Lindbergh's visits to Cain Hoy appear to have been limited. On a visit in March 1953, Guggenheim and Lindbergh went fishing in the waters around Daniel Island, and Lindbergh left behind a design for a boson's chair for Guggenheim's boat that would be "easier on the back" than its existing hard-backed seats.

Daniel Island as a Cattle Farm

Guggenheim had purchased the lower two thirds of Daniel Island in 1946 with the intention of turning the agricultural fields into pasture. This was in keeping with a pattern of land use on other hunting preserves, where timber or agriculture provided enough income to keep the rest of the land suitable for hunting. The timber industry was cyclic in its profitability, and the price of timber frequently fluctuated enough to jeopardize the flow of revenue. Landowners often sought to diversify, expanding into field agriculture and cattle farming. Guggenheim was no doubt aware of the hard times that truck farming had undergone locally, and so turned instead to establishing a cattle operation with the same vigor and precision with which he had attacked all endeavors in his life.

Truck-farming operations were immediately ceased, and the culture and landscape of the island began to be modified to meet the needs of cattle ranching. Guggenheim filled many of the drainage ditches and graded and straightened the existing roads. He also sought the support of the South Carolina Agricultural Service to find the best types of grass to support cattle ranching. Dallis grass, Dutch white clover, and lespedea were grown for summer and Ladino clover and Kentucky fescue #31 were sown for the winter months. Lighter, sandier areas such as those found on the southern end of the island were planted in crimson clover.

An inventory of the property conducted on June 30, 1947 provides an interesting glimpse into the equipment and animals that had been acquired in

Guggenheim's children and grandchildren also spent some of their Christmas or spring holidays at the Cain Hoy Plantation. Carol Langstaff is pictured here with Guggenheim in December 1958. (Courtesy the Daniel Island Company.)

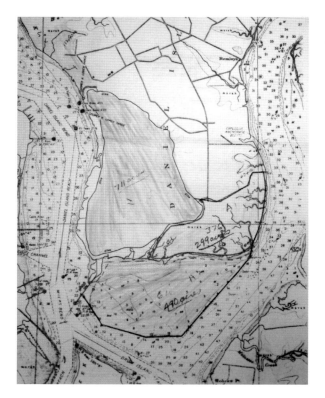

This chart was used by Henry Smythe to show Guggenheim the areas under consideration during the 1964 negotiations for extension of easements originally granted in 1953. The 790-acre area to the west was in use then but nearing capacity. The 490-acre area to the south and the 299-acre area to the east required the construction of new 10-foot dikes and the granting of additional easements. (Courtesy Library of Congress.)

the 13 months since Guggenheim had purchased the island. The property was worth $36,000 with $18,000 in livestock. This included approximately 220 cows and bulls that had been acquired within one year plus two dozen pigs. Guggenheim worked with the country's premier animal husbandry programs to increase cattle production, testing various drugs and hormones to provide optimal conditions to fatten his livestock for market. By the early 1950s he was purchasing cattle from Florida and Arizona and allowing them to reach optimal weight for sale at market. Guggenheim also had a 20,000-pound capacity truck scale built in early 1949 to allow him to more accurately weigh cattle as they were brought to the ranch and as they left the ranch for market.

The labor needs of a cattle ranch are significantly less than those of a truck farm, and within a few years of Guggenheim's 1946 purchase of lower Daniel Island only a few buildings noted on the 1947 inventory remained. Those who had lived and worked on the island were allowed to disassemble their homes and have them rebuilt on Thomas Island. The pier at Mitchell, once the heart of the truck-farming operations, along with one warehouse, are visible in USDA aerial photography from 1949 and appear to have remained operational for a while. But the next available aerial photograph, from 1957, shows the pier in ruins and no traces of the warehouse.

River Dredge Spoil adds High Land to Daniel Island

Increased shipping to Charleston after World War II and the use of deeper-draft ships necessitated an aggressive dredging program by the U.S. Army Corps of Engineers to maintain the channels. Normally, dredged material was pumped onto an adjacent piece of land. The magnitude of the dredging that was envisioned in Charleston, as well as a need to contain the spoil material so that it did not wash back into the river, led the corps to come up with a first-of-a-kind approach that involved building dikes up to 10 feet high and pumping the dredged material into the enclosed area. The intent was to both prevent having to re-dredge the same materials again and to provide a long term despoliation area that would eventually create new high land suitable for agricultural use.

Two sites were selected, one on Guggenheim's land on Daniel Island that was primarily a mix of marsh and small islands, and another on Drum Island, which was owned by the Atlantic Coast Line Railroad. On February 5, 1953, Guggenheim agreed to provide a 10-year easement to the corps of engineers for all marsh to the west and south of Daniel Island for use as

The first spoil area to the west of Daniel Island created horrific mosquito problems for Guggenheim. The water did not drain rapidly after rains, and the cracks visible in this 1963 image created ideal breeding conditions for the mosquitoes. At times, lands to the south of the island were abandoned because of the severity of the problem. (Courtesy Library of Congress.)

Active use of the first spoil area west of Daniel Island stopped in 1968. By 1972, 700 acres of the 790 were under active cultivation. This area remained agriculturally active until the last crops were planted in 1999. The South Carolina State Port Authority purchased this land in 1992 for $7 million.

dredge spoil retention areas. In May 1953, the corps started building the dikes that would enclose nearly a square mile, or 790 acres.

The dike was completed in late 1953, and the corps actively used this area for dredge spoil until 1968. Almost as soon as pumping commenced, however, the poor drainage of the site and the deep mud cracks that occurred as the spoil dried out created ideal conditions for mosquito breeding. By the late 1950s the mosquitoes were so thick that the southern cattle areas had to be abandoned for months at a time. Attempts to resolve the problem by ditching the area to allow more rapid drainage and over-spraying by aircraft were for the most part not successful and it was not until dredging stopped and the land was allowed to grow a cover of foliage that the problem abated.

In 1963, as the original easement was about to expire, the corps of engineers began negotiations with Guggenheim to both extend the lease on the existing spoil area and create additional areas. Chief concerns were the need to control the mosquito problem, and the need for the federal government to test the high land created in the first area to ensure suitability for future use as cropland or pasture land. It was envisioned that material from the shipping channels from Shipyard Creek south to the anchorage basin off Fort Sumter would be pumped into the newly created area, which would have an overall "life" of 10 years.

By late 1964, these negotiations were completed. Two additional spoil areas were to be created by the construction of 10-foot dikes. One enclosed 299 acres of marshland owned by Guggenheim on the eastern side of Daniel Island. The second enclosed 490 acres of shallow water south of the island. They were not completed, however, until 1968, which required the continued use of the first spoil area beyond the previously envisioned closure in 1965. These areas combined to add nearly an additional square mile of land to the island, and created the shape of present-day Daniel Island.

In 1975, the corps began to enlarge the dikes, raising them to 20 feet above mean low water. This extended the useful life of these areas, and allowed dredge spoil removed during the development of the Wando Welsh Terminal to be disposed of without having to create new spoil areas or obtain permits to dump the materials into the ocean off Charleston. Today the southernmost area is still actively used, but on a limited basis, by the state's port authority for dredging around the Daniel Island waterways.

The quantity of mud and sand deposited on Daniel Island over the past 50 years has been enough to cover peninsular Charleston to a depth of nearly eight

Pictured is the southern spoil area in 1995. Additional dredging was taking place at the time, adding material to the southwestern portion. The old Cooper River bridges are in the background. (Courtesy the Daniel Island Company.)

A cattle corral, two grain silos, a deep well, and this truck scale were built near the present-day intersection of Woodford and Delahow Streets. Cattle were weighed as they came onto the ranch and again when they left for the market. This 10-ton Howe truck scale remained hidden under a deep layer of leaves until recently, when the deck planking rotted away.

feet. While a part of this may be attributed to the normal maintenance associated with keeping navigation channels open, a major contributor to the rapid silting and subsequent need to dredge was created by the corps of engineers itself.

In the early 1930s, one of the country's largest hydroelectric projects was commenced in upstate South Carolina. A dam was built across the Santee River, creating Lake Marion. A diversion canal was also built to channel the waters from Lake Marion to Lake Moultrie. A dam and hydroelectric generation complex was constructed at the southern end of Lake Moultrie near Pinnopolis. Up to 128 megawatts of electrical power could be produced by the 35-foot drop and the combined flow of the Santee and Cooper Rivers. All the water that passed through the complex was channeled to the Cooper River.

The effects on the Cooper River watershed were tremendous. Prior to this diversion, the Cooper was a smaller, tidal river with brackish water and little volume flow. The addition of the Santee's water created a much larger flow of fresh water, changing the aquatic habitats all along the river. More significantly, the excessive flow resulted in severe sedimentation of the harbor and the dredged channels. These effects were already being seen in the early 1950s, and by the time the second set of easements were obtained, the corps of engineers was looking for a more permanent solution than the continued creation of dredge spoil areas. By the early 1980s a solution was designed and funded by Congress, and in 1984 a diversion project was competed that created a second hydroelectric plant whose water empties into the Santee. This has had the positive effect of restoring much of the lost flow to the Santee and reducing the volume of water in the Cooper, slowing the rate of silt accumulation in the harbor and its channels.

The Furman Track

Guggenheim was always interested in expanding his holdings in the Lowcountry. His correspondence with Victor Barringer, who had been instrumental in obtaining the Cain Hoy plantation lands in the 1930s and with whom Guggenheim maintained an active timbering partnership, details the many sites considered across the region. These were primarily timber lands that would add to his successful timber workings at Cain Hoy. Correspondence with Alistair Furman began in the early 1950s. The addition of the Furman Track would add over 1,000 acres of high lands and salt marsh immediately to the north of Guggenheim's existing holdings on Daniel Island. This would give Guggenheim ownership of all of Daniel Island, and more importantly, allowed him to expand his cattle operations.

Pictured are author Michael Dahlman Jr. and Peter Lawson-Johnston in the living room at Cain Hoy Plantation. Lawson-Johnston is the chairman of the Harry Frank Guggenheim Foundation and spent several hours with the authors providing insight and background on the history of Cain Hoy Plantation and Daniel Island.

The deer stand was used for hunting and was located near the Mitchell Pier complex.

The Furman Track had been in the Furman Family since 1878. Its main products were sea island cotton and timber, with some truck farming in the first decades of the 20th century. A 1927 pine harvest had left the land bare and the soil poor, and by the 1940s, aerial photographs show the Furman Track to be mostly devoid of any productive agricultural activity. Alistair Furman attempted to regenerate a pine forest with the planting of thousands of seedlings in the late 1940s, but these were killed in a fire started by some of the residents trying to clear land of scrub brush to create usable pasture land for their cattle. In 1951, Furman completed a project under the supervision of the U.S. Soil Conservation Service that dug over eight miles of drainage ditches to improve the arability of his land. This created 524 acres that were now in a good enough condition to support agriculture, and it was estimated that several hundred additional acres could be brought into production after clearing of light scrub brush and trees.

An agreement between Guggenheim and Furman was reached in 1955, and on October 27, Guggenheim purchased the Furman Track, which surveyors had found to consist of 702 acres of high lands and 404 acres of marsh plus a few upland islands, for $70,000. In a letter to Furman dated November 7, 1955, he expressed his desire to turn the whole of Daniel Island into one of the most "interesting cattle developments on a comparatively small scale in the country." As with his earlier purchase of Daniel Island lands, the labor needed to run the expanded farm was minimal and so he had the eight remaining families move off the island.

In 1969, knowing that he had cancer, Guggenheim began to transfer responsibilities and assets to others. Peter Lawson-Johnston, a cousin of Guggenheim, took the reins of both the Guggenheim Foundation and the operations of Cain Hoy plantation. Cattle farming was stopped on most of the island in late 1969, and the remaining cattle sold off for over $1 million.

When Guggenheim died January 20, 1971, the Cain Hoy plantation was put into a trust for Peter Lawson-Johnston, who will own the plantation until his death, at which time it will revert to the Guggenheim Foundation. The original area Guggenheim purchased in 1946 was returned to leased truck farming, with the primary crops being tomatoes and cucumbers. Migrant Hispanic labor was employed as the primary workforce, with large tractors used for all the work except harvesting. In the final years of farming, corn was introduced, which caused a tremendous growth in the island's deer and turkey populations. The northern part, still referred to as the Furman Track, was kept as a cattle farm by John Murray, who had been the island's caretaker since 1960. He maintained a cattle farm there until the early 1990s, when this land also briefly reverted to farming.

Deer hunting was an exclusive opportunity limited to those who were invited by Daniel Island landowners. This shed was built near the southern end of present-day Smythe Park to allow for the skinning and rendering of the deer. The sign on the door reads "Daniel Island Town Hall" and is currently hanging in the foyer of the Daniel Island Development Company. (Courtesy Brockington and Associates.)

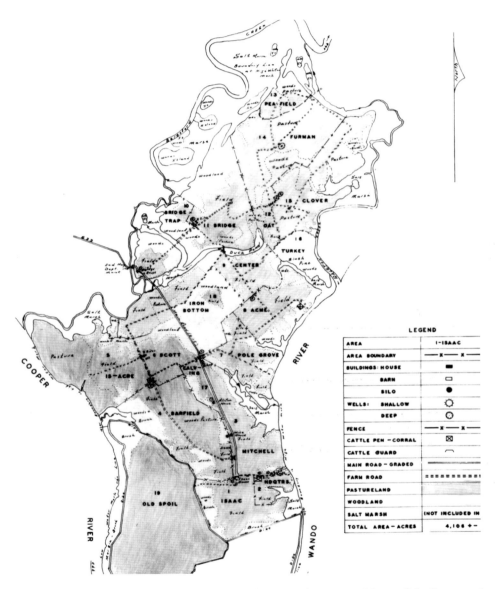

This map shows all the named farm areas as they existed in 1972. Many of the farms and their names have remained unchanged since their first use by George Cunningham in the 1880s. This plat was created to support the transfer of Daniel Island from Guggenheim's estate to the Guggenheim Foundation. (Courtesy Harry Frank Guggenheim Foundation.)

10. The Fifth Reincarnation: Daniel Island Today

Daniel Island's history has been greatly influenced by its strategic location between the Cooper and Wando Rivers. Although close to a large population center, the island was for a long time hard to get to, requiring a boat or ferry until 1940. Even with the first bridges, the area roads connected the island to the rest of the region via a round-about route. All of that began to change in 1972 when I-526, the Mark Clark Expressway, a beltway system that would cross Daniel Island and directly link it to the rest of the region, was first being planned. The winds of change blew harder in the early 1990s as construction was completed on the Wando and Don Holt Bridges.

Daniel Island was about to begin its fifth reincarnation. The first occured when the island shifted from Indian settlements and hunting lands to slave labor plantations, then to sharecropping under Cunningham. The large truck farms of the early 20th century were the island's third reincarnation, followed by Guggenheim's cattle ranching. With the building of the new bridges Daniel Island was poised to reincarnate itself for a fifth time, this time as a new town with homes and businesses.

Many potential investors approached the Harry F. Guggenheim Foundation about purchasing their holdings on Daniel Island. The foundation, content to hold the land in its natural and undeveloped state, consistently refused. By the late 1980s, however, the Guggenheim Foundation had a clear understanding that Daniel Island would eventually change. It created an ambitious development plan and was courted by the City of Charleston, the City of Mount Pleasant, and the City of North Charleston for annexation. The South Carolina State Ports Authority was also emerging as a key player in Daniel Island's future, as it considered the large expanse of land adjacent to two deep rivers as the next logical area for expanding Charleston's port infrastructure.

Daniel Island Annexed

On December 28, 1990, the announcement that the City of Charleston had voted to annex Rodent Island, Parker Island, and Daniel Island exclusive of

This gate with a "gattling gun" lock arrangement controlled access to different parts of Daniel Island from the mid 1940s to the present. It was first located near St. Jogues Island, and then as development proceeded in the 1990s it was moved several times. Its present location controls access to State Ports Authority land via a dirt road on the southern end of the island.

the southern part of the island, which was still being used for active dredge spoil deposits, forced the Guggenheim Foundation to make a decision about its future much earlier than it had anticipated. The state annexation law required that 75 percent of the owners who control more than 75 percent of the assessed value of the land be parties to the petition to be annexed by a city. The owners of Rodent Island (now called Rhoden Island) and Parker Island had to be party to this annexation, and some accounts say they were part of a political solution that Charleston mayor Joseph P. Riley desperately needed.

Mayor Riley considered the annexation of Daniel Island to be a critical part of his vision for Charleston. The land would provide additional tax base for the city, housing for a "middle class" (as most of the city was either poor or wealthy), and opportunities for new businesses. The existing city was fully developed, with no large tracts of open land for new businesses that could provide service jobs and expand opportunities beyond the medical, military, and tourism industries.

Dr. James M. Hester, the president of the Guggenheim Foundation at the time, expressed surprise at Charleston's announcement and threatened to stop the annexation in court. Mount Pleasant and North Charleston officials were also dismayed by Mayor Riley's announcement. The Guggenheim Foundation elected not to sue and instead asked the Charleston City Council to delay a decision so it could undertake its own due-diligence process.

The foundation turned to the firm of Hamilton-Rabinovitz and Alschuler for guidance and understanding of how to best respond. Over the next year, meetings took place between the Guggenheim Foundation and the cities of Charleston, North Charleston, and Mount Pleasant. Finally, on February 22, 1991, the foundation agreed to petition the city to be annexed. The decision was based on many factors but was essentially made to further the best interests of the Guggenheim Foundation. The City of Charleston offered stable political leadership and a common vision of how the island should be developed. The city promised to provide sewerage and water service, a $15 million project in late 1992, and also pledged to provide municipal buildings and to build some of the island's parks, including a large one on the southern spoil areas. Currently, the city holds 99 acres in the spoil area that extends from the Wando to the west-central part of the island. Perhaps most importantly, the Guggenheim Foundation believed that a Charleston address, and the chance to build a "city within a city," would provide the optimal conditions for the eventual development of their land at Cain Hoy.

Eight grain silos were built on Daniel Island to support cattle ranching from 1946 through the 1990s. Most of these were demolished in the early 1970s after Guggenheim's death when the lower two-thirds of the island were returned to vegetable farming. By 1995, only this silo remained, which was located on Island Park Drive near the present-day location of the Doodlebug store. (Courtesy the Daniel Island Company.)

In 1995, the Charleston Public Works Department started construction of the sewage-treatment plant for Daniel Island. The Charleston Naval Base piers are visible in the background. By 1995 the base had seen its submarines, minesweepers, tenders, destroyers, and cruisers transfered to other ports along the east coast. (Courtesy the Daniel Island Company.)

In 1992, the State Ports Authority (SPA) purchased 800 acres of former spoil land to the west and south of the island for $7 million. This was the first of several land purchases on Daniel Island and Thomas Island to the north that would be required to build the SPA's envisioned megaport in the Charleston area. In mid-June of the same year, the Mark Clark opened, including an interchange on Clements Ferry Road. Daniel Island was now easily accessible from Mount Pleasant and Charleston.

Daniel Island Company

As the Guggenheim Foundation began to consider how the island should be developed, it also considered the legal entity that would oversee the process. Prior to the opening of the Mark Clark there was little real value in the land other than for agriculture. With development on the horizon, however, the island's potential as a profit center was evident. Tax laws that governed the nonprofit foundation required that a percentage of its overall assets be spent on research and other charitable activities and stipulated that it could not have a controlling interest in a profit-making enterprise. Because of this, the foundation quickly realized that it would eventually need to sell the property. In the interim, the Daniel Island Development Company was formed by the foundation as a separate, private entity to start development activities.

The foundation assembled a team that included some of the nation's most prominent urban planners to help develop a master plan for the island. This plan was to outline guidelines for the establishment of a new town that would develop logically as a natural extension of the City of Charleston and respect the history and heritage of the region. Its design was to be based on some of the country's best, older traditional planned towns and communities, blending the best of both aesthetics and functionality. It was desired that the community's design depart from the generally accepted approach to suburban development at the time, which often involved detached subdivisions, the use of cul-de-sacs, and little, if any, attempt to incorporate mixed uses and create a sense of community. Key elements of the final master plan for Daniel Island included the incorporation of diverse housing opportunities, a central business district, a network of parks and open greenspaces, ecological protection, and

The Mark Clark Expressway opened in 1992 and enabled easy access to Daniel Island from both Mount Pleasant and Charleston. This photograph, taken in August 1995, shows the view looking east toward the Wando River and Mount Pleasant. The Daniel Island exchange would open here in 1999. To the right of the highway is the present-day location of the Town Center and the Family Circle Tennis Center. (Courtesy the Daniel Island Company.)

Until the Daniel Island exchange was completed in 1999, the only way onto the island was via the road and bridges that the state had built in 1939. In 1995, Daniel Island Drive was rebuilt and new bridges constructed over the Beresford Creek. This view looks south along Daniel Island Drive. To the left is St. Jogues Island, the future location of Blackbaud and Blackbaud stadium. (Courtesy the Daniel Island Company.)

the establishment of traditional neighborhoods with sidewalks and street trees emphasizing pedestrian activity.

It was also determined that Daniel Island should look like it evolved from the historic tradition of the Carolina Lowcountry. Civic goals included ensuring that 10 percent of the proceeds from development would go into a fund to build affordable housing (this was reduced to 5 percent in 1997), and supporting the community at large with donation of land for schools, places of worship, parks, and the arts.

The Master Pan was submitted to the City of Charleston on November 11, 1992. The first permits were pulled in 1994, and infrastructure work began in 1995 with construction of the sewer pumping station, followed by the establishment of the first homes in Codner Ferry Park, Daniel Island's first neighborhood. In May 1996, the first residents moved into the first homes on Brady Street. Matt Sloan, president of the Daniel Island Company, remembered the exhilaration of leaving the island with "one light on" for the first time since development began. Development continued at a pace dictated by the ability to sell homes and attract business to the island.

In 1997, Frank W. Brumley and Matthew R. Sloan formed the Daniel Island Company to serve as the master development company for Daniel Island, and on June 25, 1997, the company purchased 3,000 acres from the Guggenheim Foundation for $12 million. This purchase, along with another SPA purchase of some 800 acres of mostly marsh and wetlands on the same day, transferred the last vestiges of physical ownership of the island away from a family and business group that had owned the island for over 50 years.

Both Brumley and Sloan had served as advisors to the Guggenheim Foundation as it formulated plans to develop the island through the 1990s. The foundation had elected to sell to "insiders" for several reasons. First, Brumley and Sloan were known entities to the foundation's board members, and they shared a common vision for the future of the island. They had also made a fair offer for the 3,000 acres. In 1997, the Charleston real estate market was unstable and was still feeling its way through the disruptions caused by the closures of the naval base and shipyard. Thousands of high-

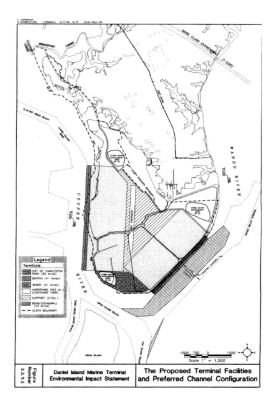

In 1999 the U.S. Army Corps of Engineers released the Draft Environmental Impact Statement for the proposed Daniel Island Terminal, later known as the Global Gateway. This schematic shows the locations of the two pier facilities that were planned by the South Carolina State Port Authority. (Courtesy U.S. Army Corps of Engineers.)

This artist's rendition shows what the proposed Daniel Island port facilities would have looked like.

paying jobs were leaving Charleston along with those ships as they transferred to other cities along the east coast.

The Global Gateway: The Marine Terminal That Almost Was

Charleston is one of the East Coast's largest commercial shipping ports, specializing primarily in container ships. Global trade continues to increase and some projections have it doubling in the next 25 years. In the early 1990s the State Ports Authority realized that it needed to start obtaining land, acquiring permits, and beginning construction that would allow the port of Charleston to meet projected demand well into the 21st century.

With the announcement of the closure of the naval base in 1993, the SPA focused on the base's land and river frontage as a near ideal location for an expansion of its port facilities. However, concerns over the expense and time needed to clean up contamination on the base, along with fears that North Charleston was becoming a dumping ground for undesirable industrial sites, and the planned use of non-union workers to handle the ships all scuttled immediate efforts to convert the base to a port facility. In early 1995, the SPA announced that another area under consideration for a new port, Daniel Island, was to be the "primary objective of [their] focus."

The ensuing battle over the Daniel Island Marine Terminal lasted until mid-2002 and polarized the region for much of that time. The SPA developed a vision for its new terminal that would have met the port's needs for most of the 21st century and that would have been the largest public works project ever undertaken in South Carolina. Called the Global Gateway, it would have provided berths for 12 ships, six on the Wando River side and six on the Cooper River side. Storage for the containers would have been provided by paving 875 acres, and 40 acres of new wharfs would have been built. New rail lines would have been constructed across Berkeley County and tied into the main rail lines north of the terminal.

Work on permitting and development of some of the infrastructure continued mostly unabated as the magnitude of the new terminal was still mostly a matter of conjecture. In 1995, the SPA purchased from the Guggenheim Foundation 210 acres on the southern part of Daniel Island, and in June 1997 it obtained another 200 acres from the foundation. Land transactions between the Daniel Island Development Company, the City of Charleston, and the SPA in June 1997 gave the SPA clear ownership of over 1,300 acres on Daniel Island.

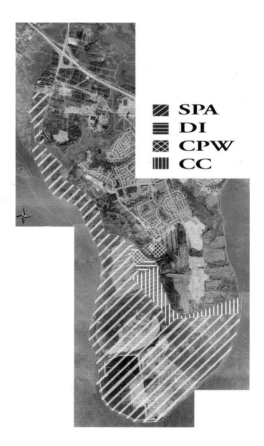

From 1995 until late 1999, the State Port Authority (SPA) purchased land along the Cooper River including a significant portion of the dredge spoil area that Guggenheim had leased to the corps of engineers in the 1950s and 1960s, as well as land that belonged to African Americans who lived on Thomas Island, in many cases on land that had been in their families since the end of the Civil War. Today, this land (represented here by diagonal cross-hatchinig) is still owned by the SPA. Other major landowners identified on this composite aerial photograph are the Daniel Island Company (DI), the Charleston Water System (CPW— formerly the Charleston Commissioners of Public Works), and the City of Charleston (CC).

SPA
DI
CPW
CC

133

The Furman Track in 1995, looking southeast toward the Wando Bridge. The northern third of Daniel Island remained a cattle farm after the death of Guggenheim in 1971 and fences subdivided this land into five farms, many of which followed the treelines seen in this photograph. Today, this land has been developed into the Ralston Creek Golf Course. (Courtesy the Daniel Island Company.)

On April 8, 1998, the SPA awarded a $7.4 million contract to construct a new highway interchange on Daniel Island. This would allow the existing interchange on Thomas Island leading to Clements Ferry Road to be the primary route for vehicular traffic to the proposed shipping terminal. This interchange opened in August 1999 and today provides the primary access to the Daniel Island community.

As plans were released and the public became more informed about the magnitude of the project, opposition developed across the region. The environmental effects of filling 41 acres of estuarine wetlands within the interior of Daniel Island, 21 acres of open water, and nearly 20 acres of wetlands along the Wando and Cooper Rivers complicated the permitting process and brought recommendations of non-approval from the South Carolina Department of Natural Resources. Homeowners along the Wando in Mount Pleasant objected to yet another major facility and the ensuing light pollution and noise that would accompany the Global Gateway. Politically, North Charleston, Charleston, and Mount Pleasant all had forceful opinions that looked to mitigate the effects on their own communities and altered several times which river would be developed first.

The Global Gateway would have also had a large effect on the Cainhoy community and the many families that lived on Thomas Island. Fred Lincoln, the chairman of the Wando Concerned Citizens Committee, spoke at the November 17, 1999 public hearing about the effects that were already being felt as land along Clouter Creek on Thomas Island was purchased by the SPA. Up to 90 properties would have to be purchased, and the SPA was authorized to begin purchasing lots in mid-1997. The owners of these lots on Thomas Island could trace them to many of the former slaves and residents of Daniel Island who had obtained land here after the Civil War and who had been displaced by Guggenheim when he converted the truck farm into a cattle ranch.

The Thomas Island lots were also being obtained by the SPA for prices significantly below market value. By August 1999, seven lots had been purchased for prices averaging under $30,000 per acre when investors and developers were paying between $170,000 and $250,000 per acre in the same area. The controversy continues today as the SPA continues to maintain ownership of these lots even though it now appears there will never be a marine terminal on Daniel Island. Fred Lincoln continues his efforts to return these lots to their previous owners.

By the end of 1999, it was apparent that the original vision of a 12-berth facility was in serious jeopardy. Political pressure was felt from both local towns and residents as well as the state legislature. Sen. Authur Ravenel co-sponsored a bill to require the SPA to obtain legislative approval for all expenditures greater than $5 million in direct response to concerns about the SPA's ability to fund the project as well as concerns over advertising and consultants that were hired at state expense to lobby the state. While the bill did not pass, it marked the beginning of opposition to the Daniel Island facility in Columbia.

State Port Authority president and CEO Bernard Groseclose continued to press for the Global Gateway in 2000, stating that if it did not acquire more space it would run out of room by 2006 or 2007. In an attempt to keep the Global Gateway project alive, the SPA in December 2000 proposed a much smaller, 500-acre terminal on the Cooper River side of the island. It also agreed to set aside an unspecified amount of land along the Wando River in a conservation easement. This new vision, although having the backing of over 20 chambers of commerce and business groups throughout the state, as well as the endorsements of North Charleston mayor Keith Sumney and Charleston mayor Joe Riley, was not well received by the community. It would have also necessitated a new environmental impact study due to the magnitude of the changes envisioned.

The Guggenheim Plaza was dedicated on November 19, 2002 and honors the life and contributions of Harry Frank Guggenheim. Eight bronze plaques explain his contributions to aviation and rocketry, his successes as a horse breeder at Cain Hoy, and his enduring vision for the community that was eventually developed on Daniel Island. The Family Circle Tennis complex is visible in the background.

In April 2002, Glenn McConnell led a successful campaign to keep the SPA from building a container terminal on Daniel Island, in part due to the effects it would have on the historically black Cainhoy community. In May 2002, then governor Jim Hodges signed a bill that directed the SPA to study sites only on the west bank of the Cooper River. In his 2002 annual state of the port address, Bernard Grossclose said, "Let me make it clear. The Ports Authority has absolutely no plans to develop a terminal on Daniel Island. While the property may have to be sold in part or in whole in the future, I believe it would be premature to do so in haste without fully analyzing its alternative value and uses."

The issue of what the SPA will do with its nearly 1,350 acres on Daniel and Thomas Islands remains under consideration today. Pristine wetlands cover a good part of the acreage along the Cooper and Wando Rivers, and there is a growing call to preserve this area for public use. Building on most of the southern part of this former dredge spoil area will also require significant investment to bring the land into productive use. Fill is notoriously unstable and tends to "liquefy" during earthquakes. It will also require massive amounts of additional fill to dry out the areas between the dikes, a problem that the SPA still had not solved during its planning for the Gateway.

Bishop England High School

In the mid-1990s, while the Daniel Island Development Company began looking for ways to help jump start development and change the perception of Daniel Island as rural farmland to a central and vibrant part of the region, Bishop England High School, located in downtown Charleston, was looking for a place where it could relocate and expand.

Bishop England is today the largest private Catholic four-year high school in South Carolina. It was founded in 1915 as a department of the Cathedral School on Queen Street. In 1916, the school was moved into an old convent building that had been donated to the school by one Mrs. Ryan of New York, on 203 Calhoun Street. It was named Bishop England at this time in honor of the first bishop of the Catholic Diocese of Charleston, John England.

England arrived in Charleston on December 30, 1820, having been consecrated the bishop of a new diocese consisting of the states of South Carolina, North Carolina, and Georgia. The few Catholics that it contained were mostly poor immigrants from Ireland or Hispaniola, but by 1832 England had grown the population of the diocese to over 11,000, with 7,500 in South Carolina alone. He particularly sought to minister to the slaves within his diocese, opening a school for black children in Charleston in 1835, which closed because of the threats of anti-abolitionist mobs.

Bishop England High School continued to grow in its city habitat, adding additional buildings in the 1940s and again in the 1960s. The beloved Reverend Robert J. Kelly became the school's rector in 1964 and helped racially integrate the school in the same year. He served as the rector until 1973 and remained an avid supporter and mentor to two more generations of Bishop England students until his death in 2004.

In the mid-1990s, when representatives from the Catholic Diocese of Charleston looked at a map and considered where current Bishop England students were living, it quickly became apparent that Daniel Island was among the lost logical and central locations for a new campus. The Daniel Island Development Company donated 40 acres to the diocese to help entice the school to move there. In September 1995, Bishop Thomson announced that the school was moving and that its current property would be sold to the College of Charleston. It helped solve both Bishop England's needs for a larger campus for its nearly 800 students, and the college's ongoing need to obtain land for its continued expansion. Construction began in 1996. David Held, who had been the assistant principal, became the new principal as the school transferred to its new home in the summer of 1998. As Philip Simmons observed, "In my day, folks left the island in order to be able to go to school. Today, they come to Daniel Island to go to school."

Family Circle Cup Tennis Complex

Since 1973, the Family Circle Cup tennis tournament had been an annual event on Hilton Head Island. In early 2000, the Charleston city economic development staff learned that the tournament was looking to move.

In the late 1990s, players were complaining that they needed time to adjust their games to the slower pace of the clay courts that the Family Circle Cup was played on. The Sea Pines Company, which hosted the tournament in Hilton Head, delayed the 1999 cup by two weeks. This did allow the players to adjust, but it also meant that the first week of qualifying coincided with the final weekend of the WorldCom Classic golf tournament. Hilton Head could not manage the resulting crowds, and this led to the tournament's search for alternative host cities.

Disney World in Orlando, suburban Cincinnati, and Stone Mountain near Atlanta were all vying for the tournament, and Charleston was a very late entrant into the race. Tournament Director Lisa Thomas learned about Daniel Island while reading a special section of the Charleston *Post and Courier* in her home in Beaufort. She wanted the event to remain in the Lowcountry, and had considered Kiawah Island at one point. But the lack of nearby hotels made Kiawah an impossibility. Daniel Island seemed to be a potentially great fit. The City of Charleston had plenty of land on the island as well as a requirement to build a tennis complex as part of the negotiations when the Guggenheim Foundation agreed to the annexation.

An agreement was signed with Gruner and Jahr Publishing, the owner of the tournament, for a 20-year commitment to hold the Family Circle Cup on Daniel Island. The city in turn financed and built a state-of-the-art circular stadium complex with 3,500 box seats, temporary seating for 6,500, plus 16 additional courts including 12 clay courts, and a 5,000 square-foot clubhouse in just over one year, in time for the 2001 tournament. Since then, the complex has provided the Lowcountry with one week of world-class tennis every year. It has also become a popular site for concerts and other cultural events, with Hootie and the Blowfish providing an annual late August evening concert.

St. Jogues Island: Home to Soccer and Software

The name Blackbaud is synonymous with Daniel Island, and the development of the software company's office complex and soccer stadium is a great example of the type of business and recreational development that Mayor Riley originally sought in the city's annexation of the island in 1990. St. Jogues Island is just northwest of Daniel Island and is today commonly considered part of Daniel Island proper. This name for the island was found on a 1726 deed of gift from Richard Codner to William and Benjamin Stuart, and was also known as Brady Island.

Michael Trinkley, the archeologist for the South Carolina Department of Transportation, conducted the initial investigations of the Elfe Plantation on St. Jogues Island in 1985. He believed Jogues to have been the French missionary Isaac Jogues, who was sent to Canada in 1636. A Roman Catholic and a member of the Society of Jesus, he worked tirelessly to preach the gospel "a thousand miles to the interior of the territory." In 1646, he was murdered as he tried to broker a peace treaty with the Iroquois. It is highly probable that the French Huguenots trying to establish themselves in the new colony of Carolina knew of his heroism and honored his work as an explorer and missionary.

In 1982, Tony Bakker founded Blackbaud Microsystems Inc. on Long Island, New York and rapidly expanded its operations. By 1987, it was the 37th-fastest-

Henry Smythe was Guggenheim's Charleston attorney and close friend and confidant. By the late 1950s, and for the remainder of Guggenheim's life, he provided clear and direct support to the Cain Hoy and Daniel Island operations. He is pictured here on Daniel Island in the 1990s. (Courtesy the Daniel Island Company.)

The Blackbaud Soccer Stadium is home to the Charleston Battery, a United Soccer League First Division professional soccer team. On October 23, 2005, over 4,000 fans watched the U.S. women's national soccer team defeat regional rival Mexico 3–0.

growing private U.S. company, according to *Inc.* magazine's annual listing. In 1989, Bakker decided to move away from New York to a new building on U.S. Highway 17 in Mount Pleasant. In 1992, the company leased most of the Ashley Center in North Charleston, but by 1997 it had grown out of its 66,000 square feet there. In late 1997, Bakker bought 37 acres on St. Jogues Island and built a 320,000-square-foot complex that the company moved into in the summer of 2000. Today Blackbaud is the leading global provider of software and related services designed specifically for nonprofit organizations.

Bakker's other passion is soccer. A native of London, he played for the University of Southampton and the University of Houston, and coached locally at the James Island Youth Soccer Club. Now firmly a resident of the Lowcountry, he established the Charleston Battery Soccer Club in 1993 with the help of a group of local investors. The Battery has been one of the United Soccer League's top competitive clubs in its 16-year history. In conjunction with the construction of the Blackbaud corporate offices in the late 1990s, Bakker led a team of investors in the design and development of a soccer stadium for his beloved Battery. In 1999, the Blackbaud Soccer Stadium opened. It was the first professional soccer-specific stadium in the United Soccer League's first division. It has 2,500 reserved armchair seats and a total seating capacity of 5,100, and the English-style Three Lions Pub features soccer memorabilia from around the world.

A Look Back

Daniel Island is undergoing its largest transformation since the Carolina colony's first settlers started occupying the island in 1671. However, it is not a transformation at odds with its history. Today's development is a process that the landowners of the past would have understood and, if they were alive today, would most likely take part in. This land has always provided for those who lived here and who sought to use its unique location and natural resources in ways that were dictated by the local, national, and international communities. The Etiwan Indians valued the island for its prolific wildlife in both marine estuaries and on higher dry land, and for its central location from which trade could be conducted and where dwellings could be built. European settlers sought the riches of its trees and its land when global demand for timber, brick, naval stores, indigo, and sea island cotton made property on the island highly desirable. In the 20th century, truck farming and cattle ranching became the mainstays of Daniel Island's production. Today, the island's most valuable asset is still its land, which can be used to create new housing and new businesses in a location ideally situated between the cities of Mount Pleasant, Charleston, and North Charleston.

This fifth reincarnation of Daniel Island is also being accomplished in a way that honors and remembers those who have lived and worked here before. Many of the features that Robert Daniell, Isaac Lesesne, George Cunningham, Harry Guggenheim, and generations of slaves would recognize are still here. The Guggenheim Foundation and the Daniel Island Company retained and worked into the structure of the master plan the rows of live oaks that marked the boundaries of the Daniel and Lesesne Plantations, and the Seven Farms that Cunningham developed in the 1800s. Many of the island's "new roads" are not that different from the public roads built and maintained by the Carolina colony in the early 18th century. The shoreline along the Wando and Cooper Rivers remains virtually unchanged north of the spoil areas on the south end of the island. Cemeteries have been cleared of decades of undergrowth, and the sites of some of the original plantations are being preserved in an undeveloped state.

It is this unique combination of historical perspective along with thousands of new residents and dozens of new businesses that makes Daniel Island the unique jewel that it is at the place where the Wando meets the Cooper.

The Lesesne graveyard is behind the Family Circle tennis complex. This marker was placed in April 2001 by descendents of Isaac Lesesne and reads, "Isaac Lesesne (1674–1736) was one of many French Huguenots who fled persecution under Louis XIV for the promise of religious tolerance and abundant land in the Carolina Provence. Perhaps as early as 1720, French settlers on Daniel Island had become an indistinguishable element of the Carolina society. Isaac Lesesne fathered eight children. Isaac Lesesne Jr. expanded the plantation's production with lime and sawmills and maintained a store in Charleston, where he lived and contributed to community projects. He participated in the political strife preceeding the American Revolution and died in 1772. But his son Isaac Walker Lesesne served as a Coronet in the cavalry, probably in Francis Marion's brigade. A century of family ownership of the Daniel Island plantation ended in 1808. But this cemetery was retained with water rights of access."

APPENDIX 1. HISTORIC CEMETERIES

The five known historic burial sites and cemeteries on the island are located along the marshes and rivers. The Lesesne Cemetery, for example, was placed next to the Wando to ensure that family members could still visit the graves by water even if the land around the site was sold. Of more immediate importance, however, was the fact that arable land on Daniel Island was a valuable resource and it did not make sense to give it up for cemeteries.

Three other sites contain the remains of African Americans who lived and worked on Daniel Island following the Civil War. They contain an identifiable total of over 150 graves, with only 50 bearing any sort of headstone or marker. In most cases, according to Reverends Dennis and Reilly, markers were made of wood that quickly rotted or the graves were outlined in shells that washed away. It is also likely that these cemeteries were used from the earliest settlements and that burials often occurred inadvertently in the same place where past generations had been buried.

Two other graves have been located on the south bank of Beresford Creek across from the former sales center in the Codner's Ferry neighborhood. Nothing is known about who may have been buried here.

The Lesesne Family Cemetery

With approximately 20 to 30 individuals and markers dating from 1778 to 1884, this cemetery contains the remains of members of the Lesesne, Beekman, Brailsford, and Parker families. Historic deeds confirm that these families were prominent planters on Daniel Island during the late 18th and early 19th centuries. This table shows the legible markings remaining on 10 surviving markers.

Name	Inscription	Born	Died
William Roper Brailsford	Confederate Veteran	10/13/1822	2/3/1871
Anna Lucia Brailsford	Died in the 86th year of her life		3/12/1884
Thomas Cochran	65 years		11/ /1803
Susan Cochran			6/5/1808
Ms. Elizabeth Beekman	In Memory of the Pious dead, this stone marks the place where are interred the remains of Ms Elizabeth Beekman who was born on Daniels Island on the 29th of January 1754 and		

This, the oldest tombstone on Daniel Island, is made of slate and is located in the Lesesne Cemetery. It bears the following inscription:

In Memory of
James Frederick Lesesne
Son of John and Mary
Lesesne, who died
August 17th, 1784
Aged 11 Months

	died in Charleston on the 21st of February 1815
Charles Beekman, Esquire	Son of Bernard and Elizabeth Beekman who was born in Charleston on 21st of August 1776 and died in the same place on February 17th 1797
Sarah Lesesne	Born on the island of New Providence on April 3rd, 1728 and died on the 19th of January 1778
Mary Lesesne	68 years 2/7/1848
James Frederick Lesesne	In Memory of James Frederick Lesesne Son of John and Mary Lesesne, who died August 17th, 1784 Aged 11 Months
Ms. Elizabeth Parker	Died in the 71st year of her life 8/6/1818 Blessed are the poor in spirit, for they shall see God
_____ Holland	Daughter of _____ and Anna F Parker Died on the 12th of November 1848 in the 54th year of her life

Lesesne African American Cemetery

This site contains the remains of approximately 45 to 50 individuals. It has 17 marked graves with a date range of 1927 to 1969. When first cataloged by Brockington and Associates, this cemetery had multiple identifiable grave depressions that were marked with whelks, ironstone dishes, pressed glass tableware, and bottles, all of which are traditional African American grave goods. Today these markers are gone, but the numerous and often deep depressions make it plausible to assume that this graveyard has in been in use since well before the 20th century.

Three World War I military markers indicate service in the 371st colored infantry regiments. Formed in August 1917 at Camp Jackson outside Columbia, the 371st was made up entirely of drafted black soldiers. By the end of the year, 3,380 men were received by the regiment, with 1,680 selected to serve in labor battalions and 500 assigned to a combat unit. In 1918, the 371st was sent to France where it fought in the trenches near Verdun and was at the center of fighting during the Great September Offensive. Despite discrimination and segregation, these soldiers proved their valor in battle after battle, and were consistently praised by French and American officers for their tenacity and courage on the battlefield.

Name	Inscription	Born	Died
Mrs. Lucielle F. Coleman	(metal marker)	1906	1965
April Shaw	PVT, US Army	7/8/1895	8/31/1958
Cupid Shaw	Deacon, Mary Ann Baptist Church	2/21/1871	1/31/1927
Hannah Shaw	53 years		6/2/1928
Ben Crews	At Rest	3/22/1903	4/7/1947
Sarah Frost		11/ /1906	4/ 7 /1927
Henry Simmons	At Rest	1884	1942
William Simmons	Company A, 346 Service Battalion, QMC World War I	4/15/1897	7/12/1961
Eva Simmons	64 years		8/15/1964
Susan Simmons	(metal marker)		12/26/1957
William Simmons	Father	1854	1941
Rosa Burns	(metal marker)		2/2/64

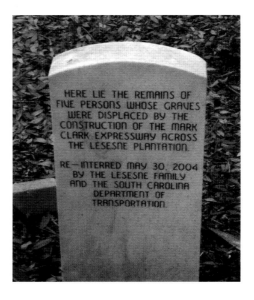

During archeological investigations of the Lesesne Plantation conducted in 1985, five bodies were in what appears to have been a 25-foot by 25-foot family plot. The three adult women, one young adult male, and one female child were reinterred on May 30, 2004. They were Caucasian and were buried in hexagonal caskets before the Civil War. The acidic soils at this location heavily deteriorated the bones. This can be contrasted to the Native American remains discovered elsewhere and well-preserved for over 500 years in neutral clay.

The banks of the Wando have eroded since the Lesesne family established a cemetery in the 18th century. Many grave markers were found in the marsh area when archeological work commenced in the mid-1980s and were placed on higher land. More stabilization work will be needed to prevent further destruction of this historic graveyard.

Edward Burns	PVC Labor Battalion USA WWI	9/10/1894	4/10/1952
Etta Perrineau			12/28/1958
Nancy Mitchell	At Rest	8/15/1872	10/8/1957
Melvin Shalls	(metal marker)		8/15/1969
Lula Williams	Born in New York She is not dead but sleepeth	1/26/1927	12/30/1935

Simmons Cemetery

Holding the remains of approximately 65 to 70 individuals, with 21 marked graves and a date range of 1905 to 1973, the Simmons Cemetery is located near the sales center and the ruins of Governor Daniell's plantation. It has long been known as the Simmons Cemetery because it was associated with a plantation owned by Maurice Simmons in the years just prior to the Civil War. Multiple identifiable grave depressions were marked with whelks and other traditional African American grave goods when first cataloged in 1985. Two World War I military markers indicate service in the black infantry regiments, and one Civil War marker identifies the grave of an African American who fought for the Union as a part of the U.S. colored infantry.

Name	Inscription	Born	Died
John Pickens	The Lord is my Sheppard, I shall not want	11/20/1833	6/2/1905
Jane Bellinger	Mother	3/23/1872	4/23/1942
John Bellinger	PVT, Company A 57th BN WWI infantry	5/6/1892	9/15/1956
Carry Haywood			
Benjamin Bellinger	49 years. May Thy Resurrection Find Thee on the Bosom of Thy God		3/13/1927
Arthur Smalls		2/4/1912	12/23/1954
Thomas Glover	PVT South Carolina 156th Depot brigade	5/28/1889	8/13/1940
Isaac Mc Coy	(metal plate)		1/21/1959
Elijah Fordham	(metal plate)		10/7/1963
Clarence Fordham	He lived the life, and kept the faith	8/31/1921	1/14/1941
Irene P. Fordham		10/26/1883	2/23/1952
Rebecca Drayton	The Lord is my Sheppard	4/15/1919	12/3/1955
Benjamin Fordham	(metal plate)		1/3/68

Left: *John Bellinger served in a combat unit that was integrated with the French troops stationed in the Verdun sector.* Right: *Edward Burns was born on Daniel Island, and according to his draft registration card from June 1918, lived just outside of Charleston. He worked for Virginia Carolina Chemicals. His mother Annie still lived on Daniel Island at the time.*

Left: *Thomas Glover was assigned to the 156th Depot Brigade in World War I. His draft registration card shows that he was born on May 28, 1889 in Awendaw, and in June 1917 was employed as a laborer on the Daniel Island truck farm. He was married with eight children.* Right: *April Shaw was born on July 28, 1895 according to his draft registration card. He lived on Clements Ferry, a name sometimes given to Thomas Island. He was not married in June 1917 and described himself as a self-employed fisherman.*

Peter Campbell	Father	4/20/1876	12/31/1938
William Campbell		1888	1955
Ernestine Venning	(metal plate)		9/13/73
G.C. Coxswain	Corporal Company K, 103 USCI		
Lorrinda B Gibbs		11/19/1900	1/18/1971
Evelina Gilliard Robinson	Your loving Children, Oscar, Lilly, Mary, Florence, Eva, Evelina, Benjamin	10/27/1907	1/9/1965
Albertha P. Jenkins			
Recer G. Jenkins	Loving Mother	4/27/1877	2/4/1956

Daniel Island Park Cemetery

This graveyard on Ralston Creek Street in Daniel Island Park contains approximately 25 to 30 individuals, and has 12 marked graves with a date range of 1898 to 1958. Many of the people buried in Daniel Island's three African American cemeteries were direct descendents of the slaves who worked the plantations and farms. Slaves were often known only by their first names, but with the end of the war and the coming of abolition, last names were needed, so families often took the names of their former owners.

Name	Inscription	Born	Died
Adolphus McCall	48 years		12/24/1914
Lousa Gethers		1860	1937
Sarah Simmons	Mother	1870	1941
Susie Drayton		12/15/1865	5/19/1898
James Denis		1886	10/5/1931
James Dennis		4/2/1904	8/22/1958
Benjamin Dennis	Age 42 (metal marker)		6/10/1952
Sara Dennis		6/9/1877	2/1/1936
Bernie Dennis		4/17/05	6/12/1952
Ida Doctor		8/5/1906	3/15/1953
Priscilla Jinkins		1831	2/14/1923
Leon Jenkins		8/15/1912	7/17/1952

William Simmons was born on Daniel Island and in June 1918 worked for the Virginia Chemical Company in Charleston. His mother Sarah and father William both lived on Daniel Island and are both buried on the island.

APPENDIX 2. AERIAL PHOTOGRAPHY

Daniel Island in 1949. Guggenheim purchased the southern areas of Daniel Island in 1946, and rapidly converted the island from truck farming to cattle ranching. Roads were straightened or removed, drainage ditches filled in, and many of the houses that had supported workers during truck farming removed. The southern part of the island is pictured before the addition of the dikes to contain dredge spoils. To the north, there is a clear demarcation of the Furman Track, which in 1949 was mostly fallow land with little agricultural value. (Courtesy U.S. Department of Agriculture.)

Daniel Island in 1957. The dikes for the dredge spoil areas were completed in 1953, and dredging operations had started to fill in the 790 acres of former marshland by the time of this photograph. Large tracts of heavily forested land in the center of the island that had been unsuitable for agriculture due to poor drainage had been cleared by this time and were in active use as pasture. The large white drainage ditiches in the upper right are on the Furman Track, and had been cut by Furman with the help of the Agriculture Cooperative in 1951 to improve drainage and make the land more productive. (Courtesy U.S. Department of Agriculture.)

Daniel Island in 1963. The spoil area was nearly full, and a groin had been added to the southwest corner to reduce the silting of the main navigation channel to the south of Daniel Island. The Furman Track to the north was now fully integrated into the cattle farm, and the large drainage ditches had been filled in. (Courtesy U.S. Department of Agriculture.)

Daniel Island in 1979. After Guggenheim's death in 1971, the lower portion of the island reverted to truck farming, while the Furman Track to the north continued as a cattle ranch under the stewardship of John Murray. The first spoil area was returned to agricultural use in 1972, and additional spoil areas expanded the island to the south into marsh and very shallow waters, encompassing an additional 800 acres. (Courtesy U.S. Department of Agriculture.)

Archeological Data Recovery at 38BK207 (Elfe Plantation) Daniel Island, South Carolina. Prepared for the Daniel Island Development Corporation. Brockington and Associates, 1998.

Archaeological Investigation of the Portion of 38BK202 in Phase II of the Proposed Family Circle Cup Tennis Complex Daniel Island, Berkeley County South Carolina. Prepared for the Family Circle Cup and the City of Charleston Department of Parks and Recreation, 2001.

Archaeological Testing of 38BK815 (which includes the site of Governor Daniell's Home site) and 38BK1625. Prepared for the Daniel Island Company Brockington and Associates, 1999, 2002.

Archaeological Testing of 38BK1626, 38BK1627, 38BK1628 and 38BK1629. Prepared for the Daniel Island Company. Brockington and Associates, 2002.

Borick, Carl P. *A Gallant Defense: The Siege of Charleston, 1780.* Columbia: University of South Carolina Press, 2003.

Brockington, Paul and Eric Poplin. *Cultural Resources Survey of Daniel Island, Berkeley County, South Carolina.* Prepared for the Daniel Island Investment Company, Charleston. Brockington and Associates, 1994.

Cultural Resource Survey of Roddin's Island 1 and 2 Berkeley County SC. Prepared for the Daniel Island Company. Brockington and Associates, 2001.

I.C.S. Reference Library, Volume 105. Section 15: Limes, Cements and Mortars. London: International Correspondence Schools, 1923.

Ibid. *Section 20: Brickwork and Manufacture of Brick.*

Lawson-Johnston, Peter. *Growing Up Guggenheim.* Wilmington, Delaware: ISI Books, 2005.

Lesesne, Thomas Petigru. *The History of Charleston County, South Carolina.* Charleston.

Miles, Suzannah Smith. *East Cooper Gazzetteer.* Charleston: History Press, 2004.

McCord, David J. *Statues at Large of South Carolina Ninth Volume, containing the Acts Relating to Roads, Bridges and Ferries*. Columbia, 1841.

Orvin, Maxwell C. *Historic Berkeley County, South Carolina (1671–1900)*. Charleston: Comprint, 1973.

Papers of Harry Guggenheim (1890–1971), The. Manuscript Division, Library of Congress, Washington D.C.

Poplin, Eric and Marian D. Roberts. *Historical and Archeological Overview of Daniel Island, Berkeley County, South Carolina*. Prepared for the Harry Frank Guggenheim Foundation and Olympia and York Companies, New York. Brockington and Associates, 1992.

Smith, Henry A. M. *The Baronies of South Carolina*. South Carolina Historical Society, 1931.

South Carolina Historical Society. *The Shaftesbury Papers*. Charleston: Tempus Publishing, 2000.

Wayne, Lucy B. *Burning Brick: A Study of a Lowcountry Industry*. Gainesville, Florida: Ph.D. dissertation, Department of Anthropology, University of Florida, 1992.

Williams, Clara Daniell. *Daniell Family History Book Two*. Alpharetta, Georgia: W. H. Wolfe Associates Historical Publishing, 1992.

Zierden, Martha A., Lesley M. Drucker, and Jeanne Calhoun. *Home Upriver: Rural life on Daniel's Island Berkeley County South Carolina*. Columbia: South Carolina Department of Transportation, 1986.